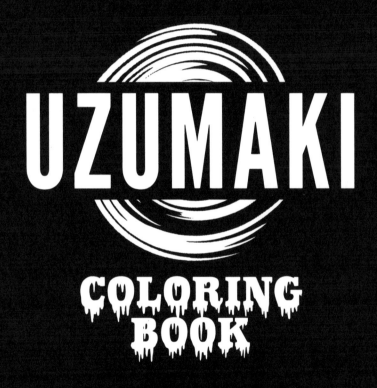

UZUMAKI

COLORING BOOK

UZUMAKI

COLORING BOOK

SELECTED ART FROM THE MANGA BY
JUNJI ITO

Touch-Up Art: Walden Wong
Cover & Graphic Design: Adam Grano
Editor: Masumi Washington

Printed in the U.S.A.

Published by VIZ Media, LLC
P.O. Box 77010
San Francisco, CA 94107

10 9 8 7 6 5 4 3 2 1
First printing, March 2022

VIZ MEDIA
viz.com

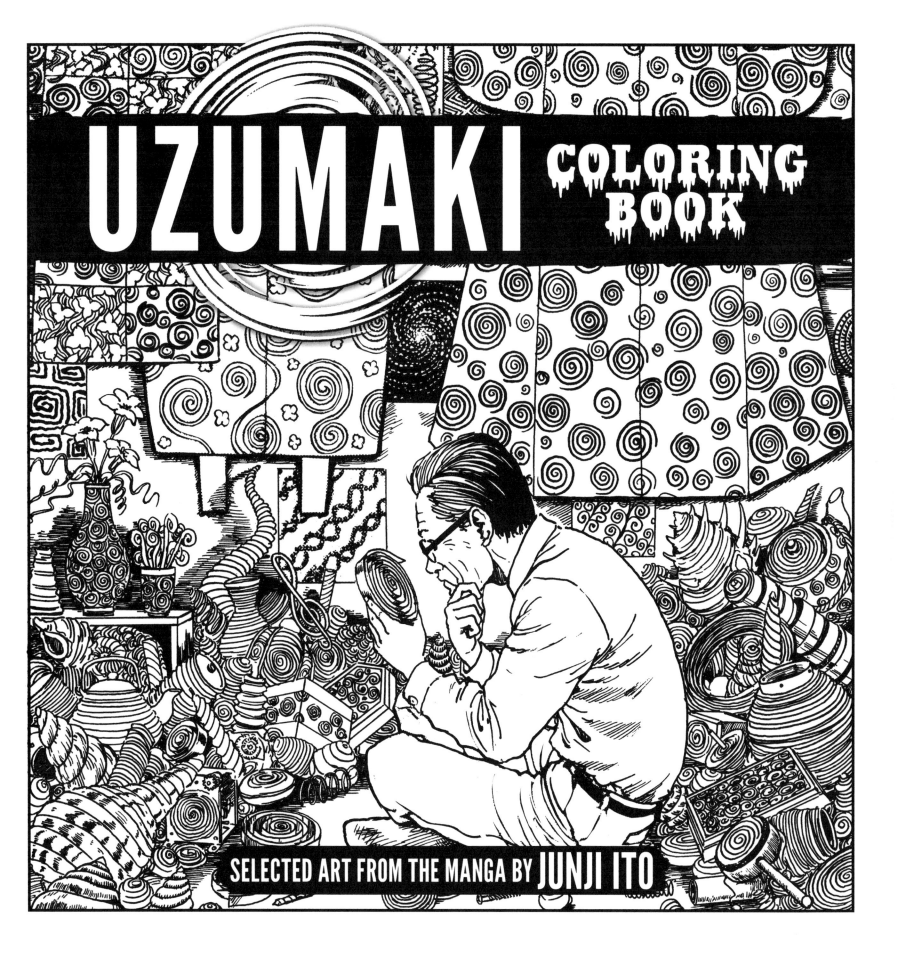

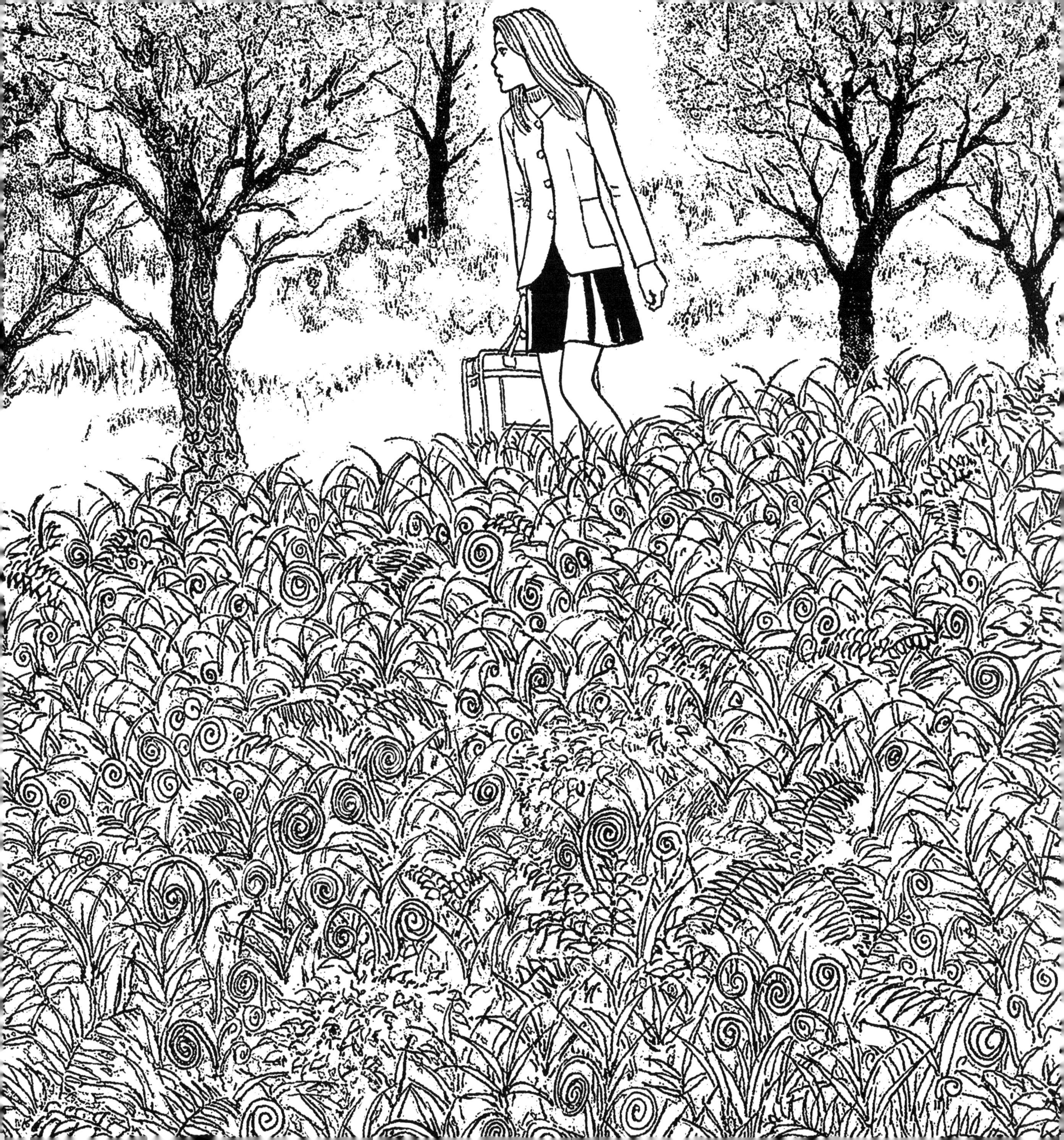

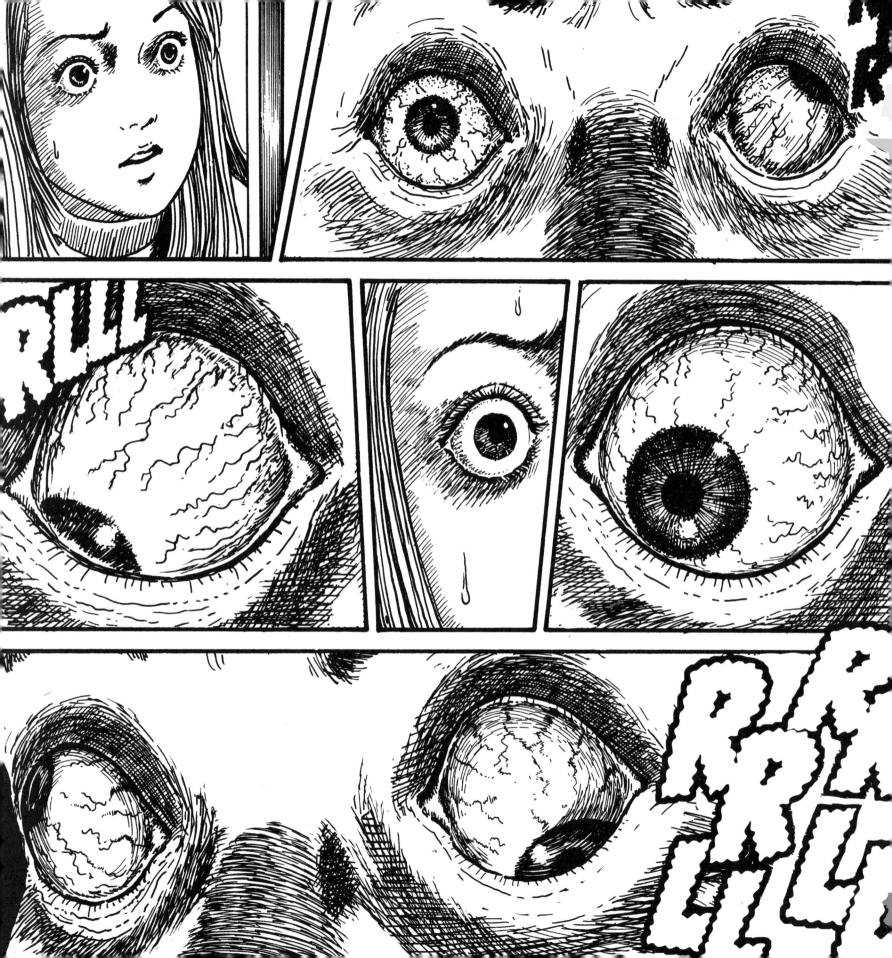

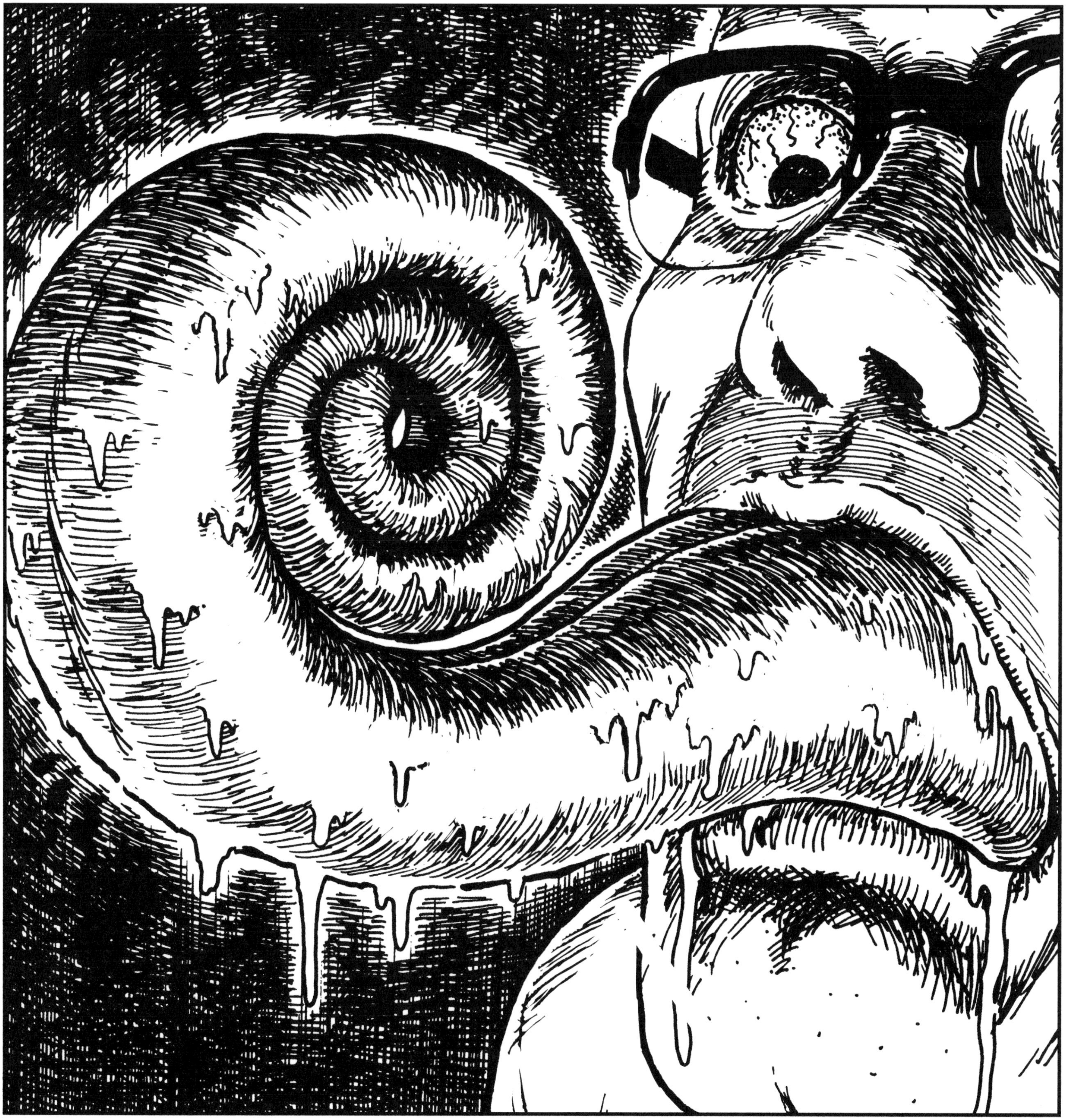

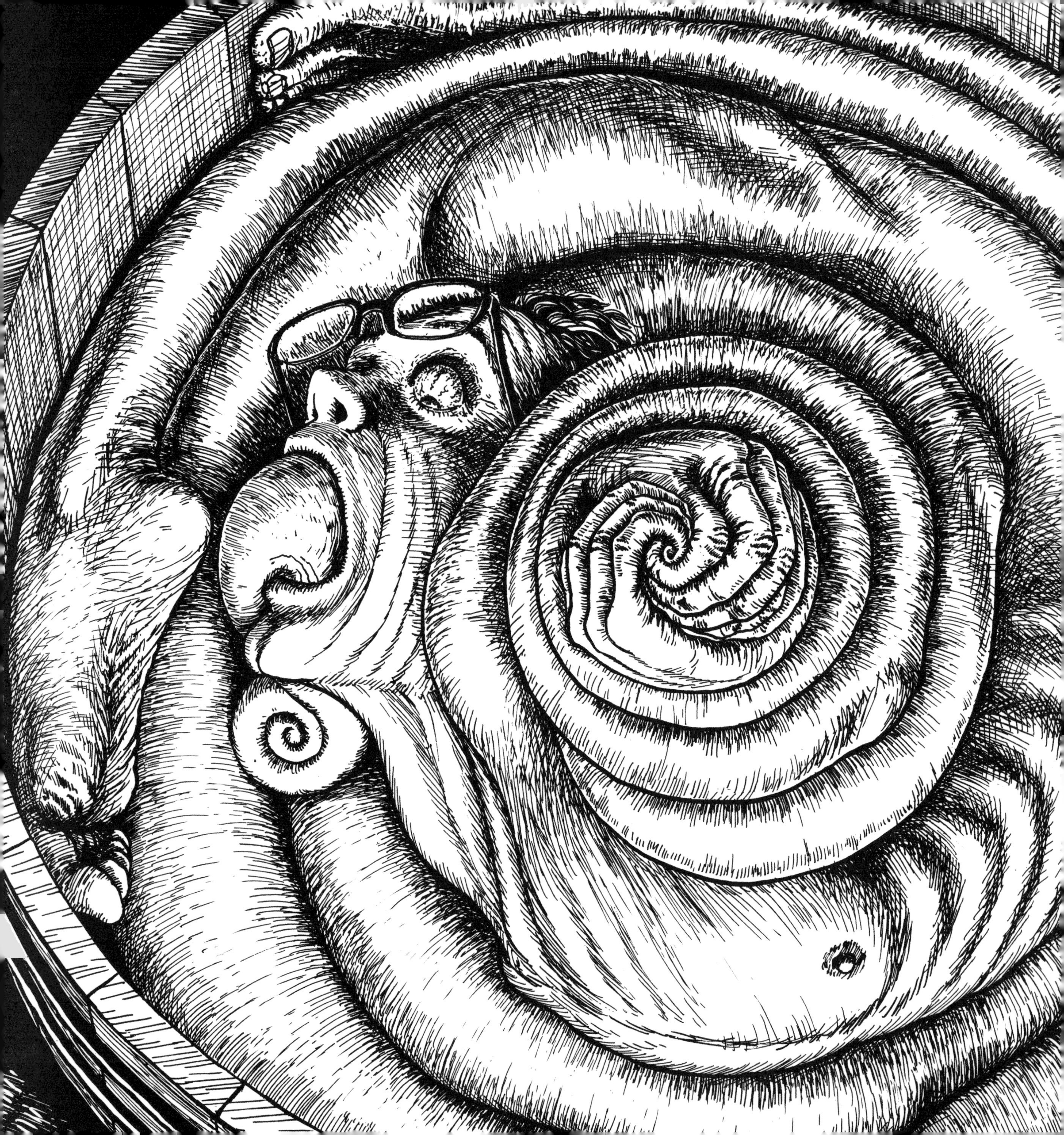

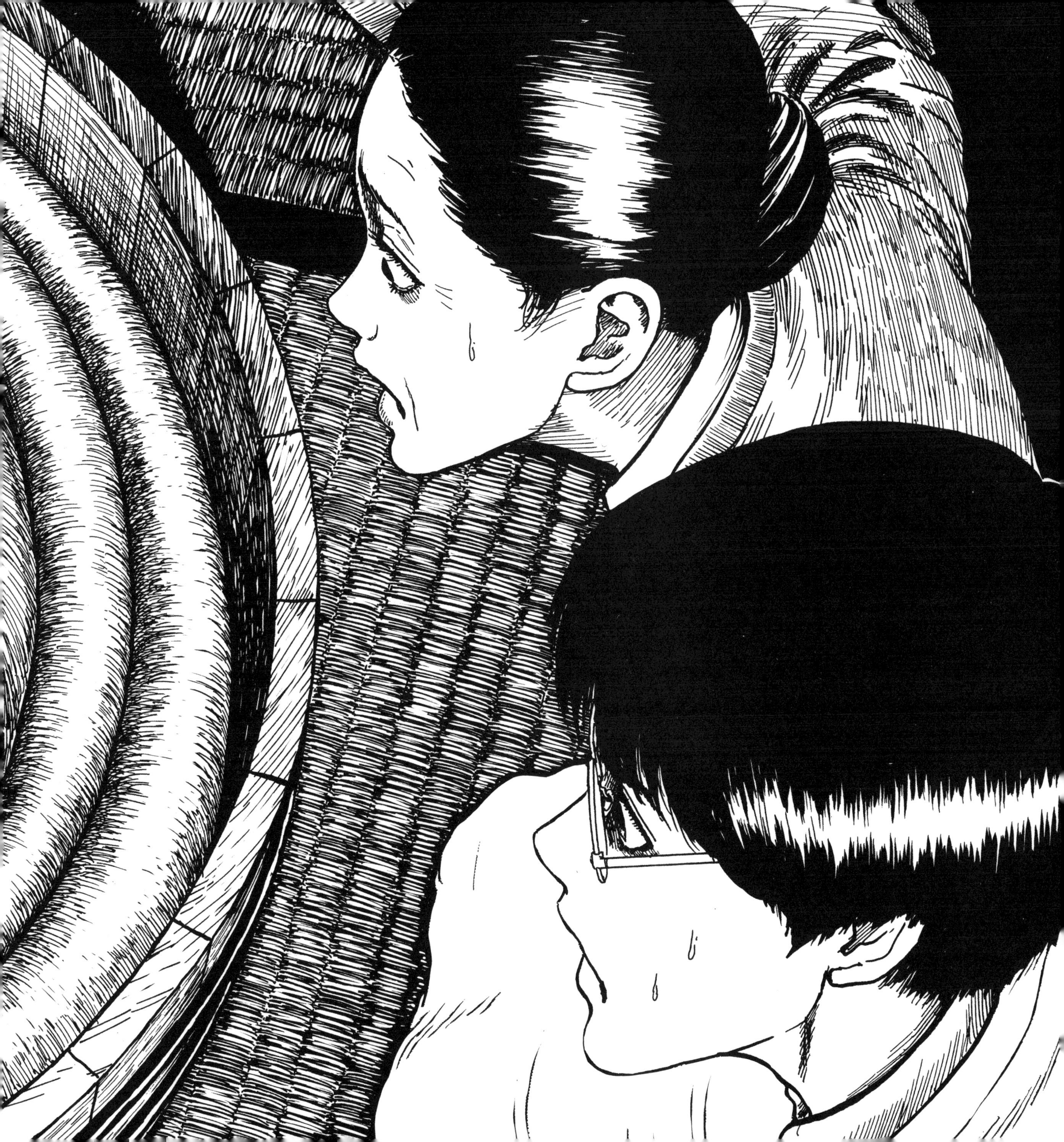

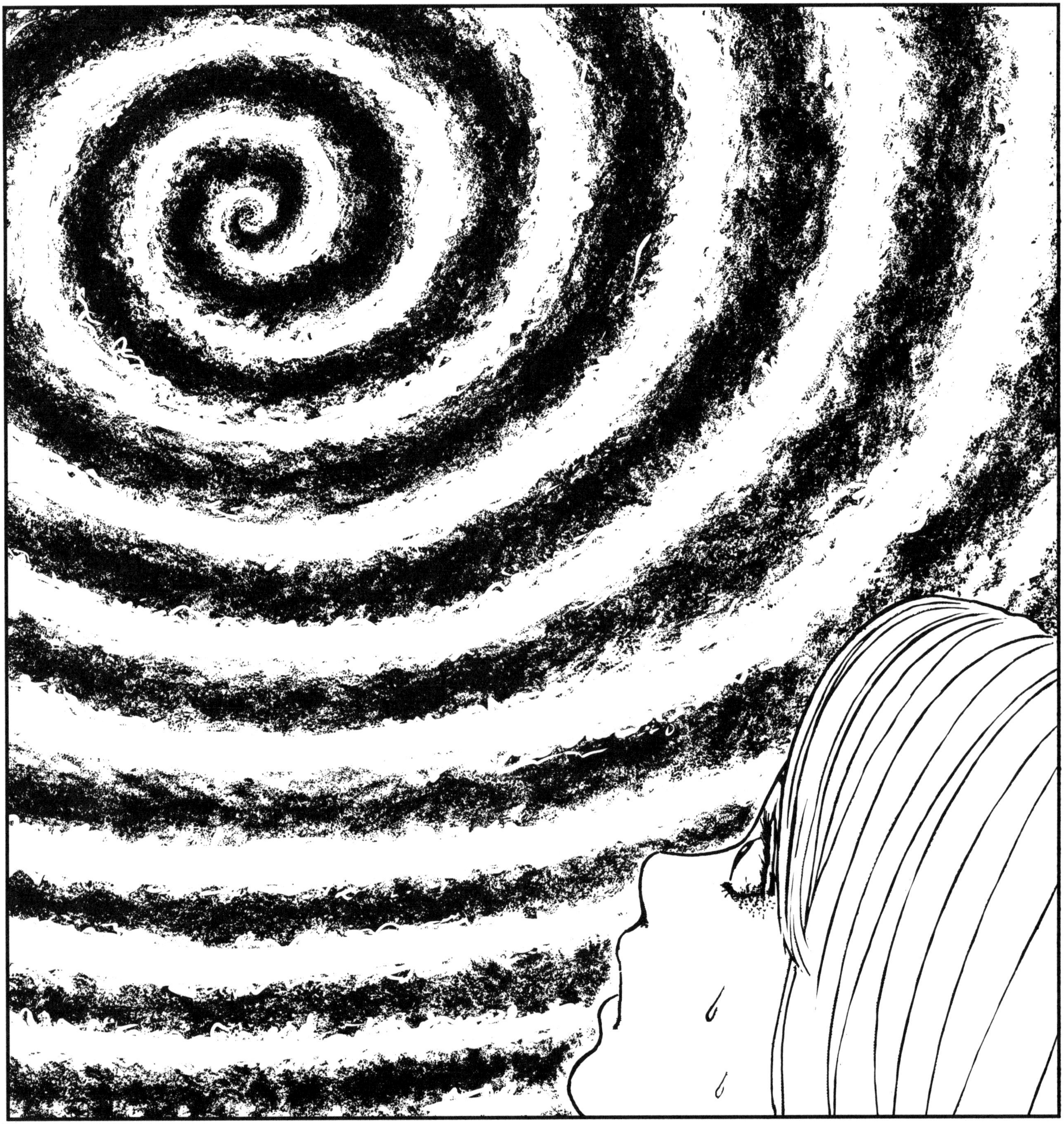

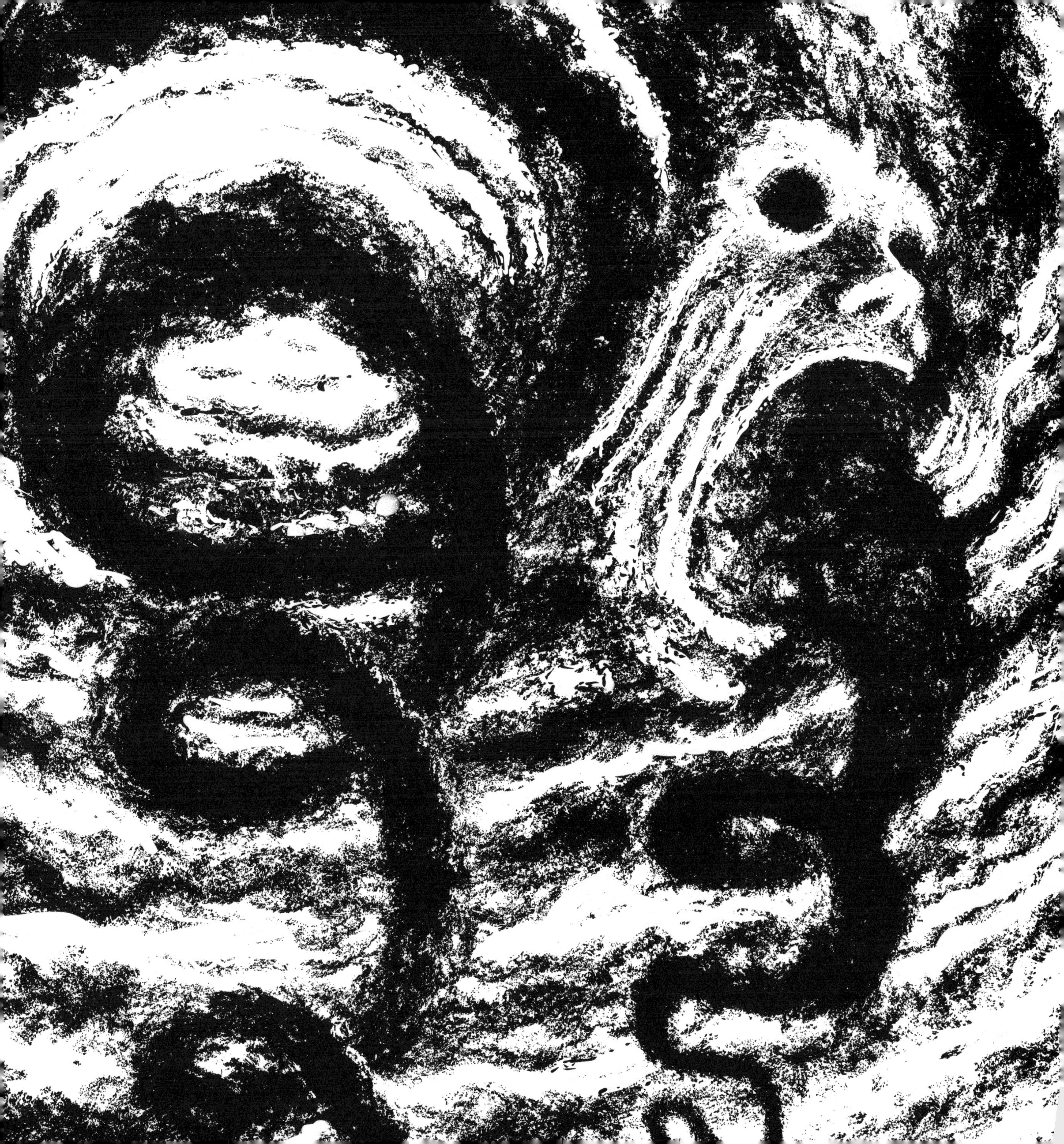

FWICH
FWINCH
FWICH

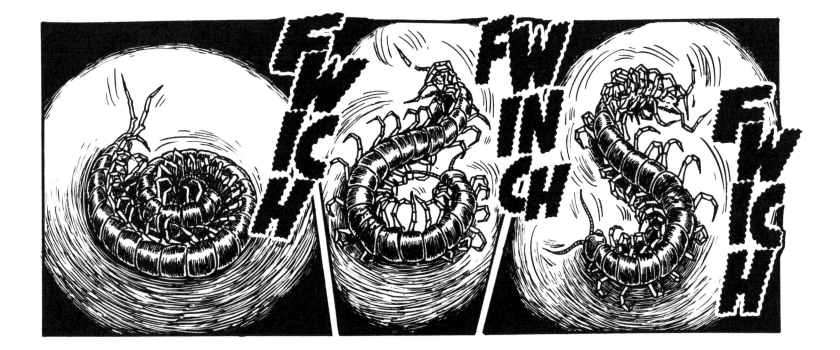

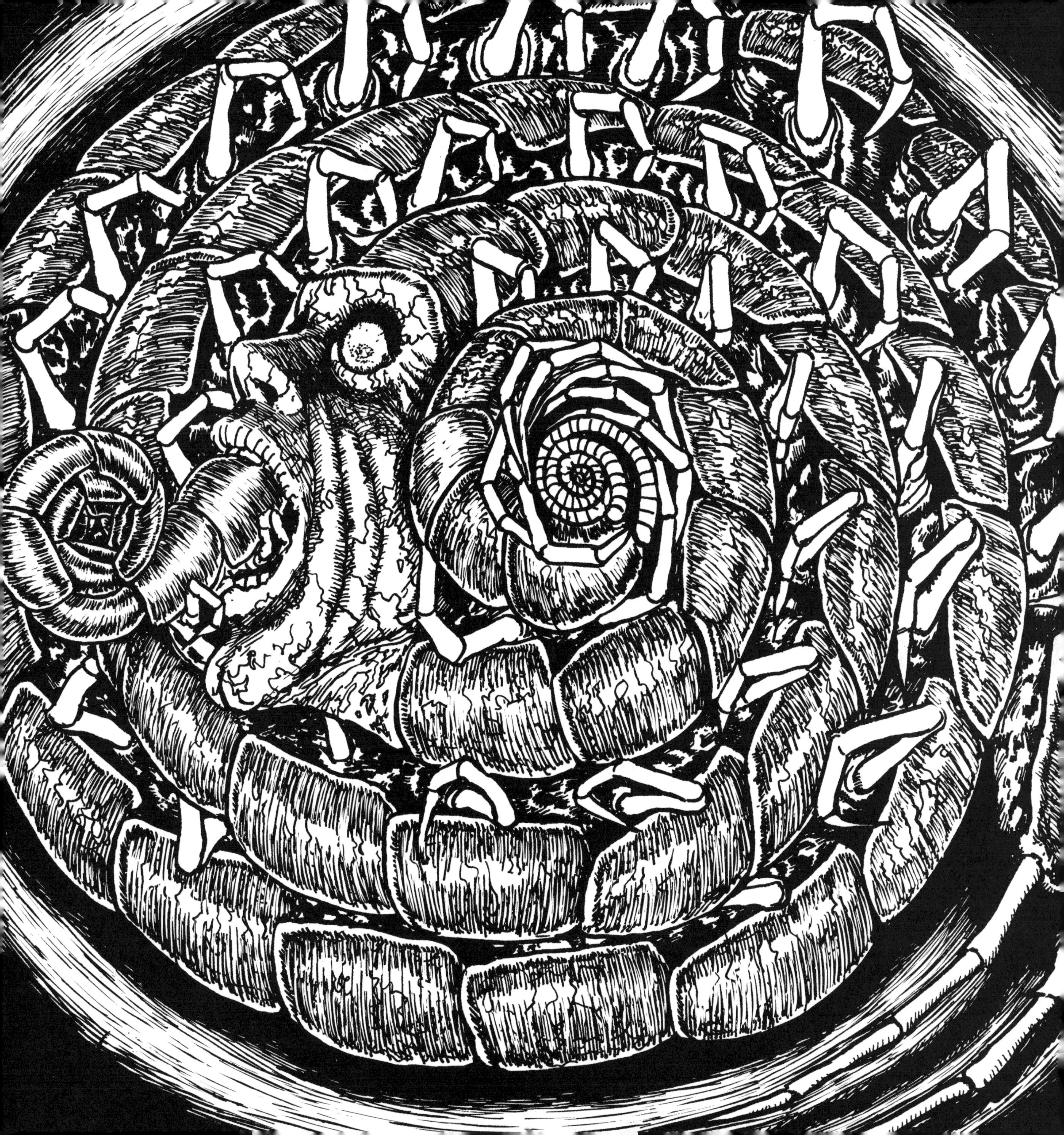

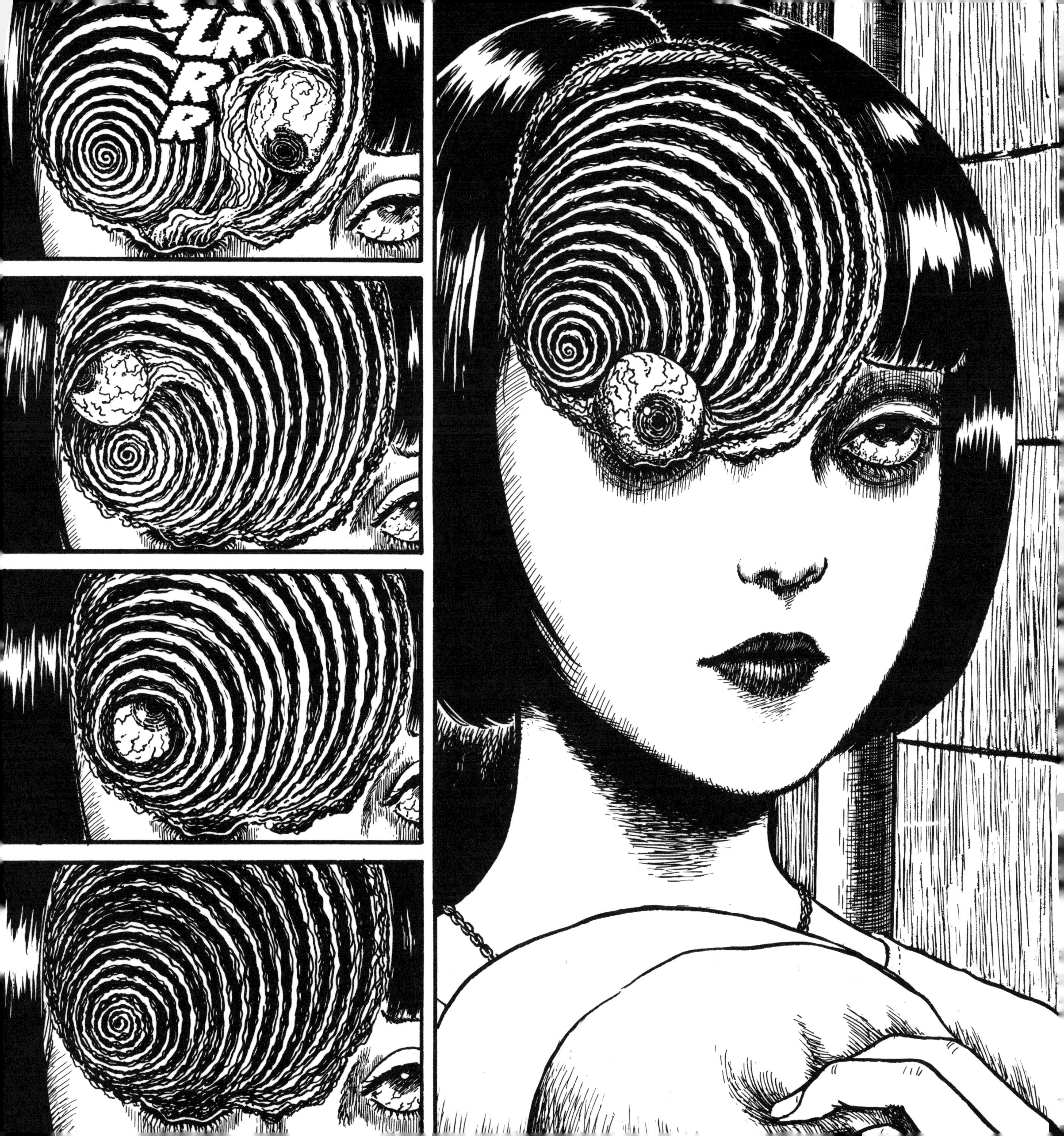
SLRRR

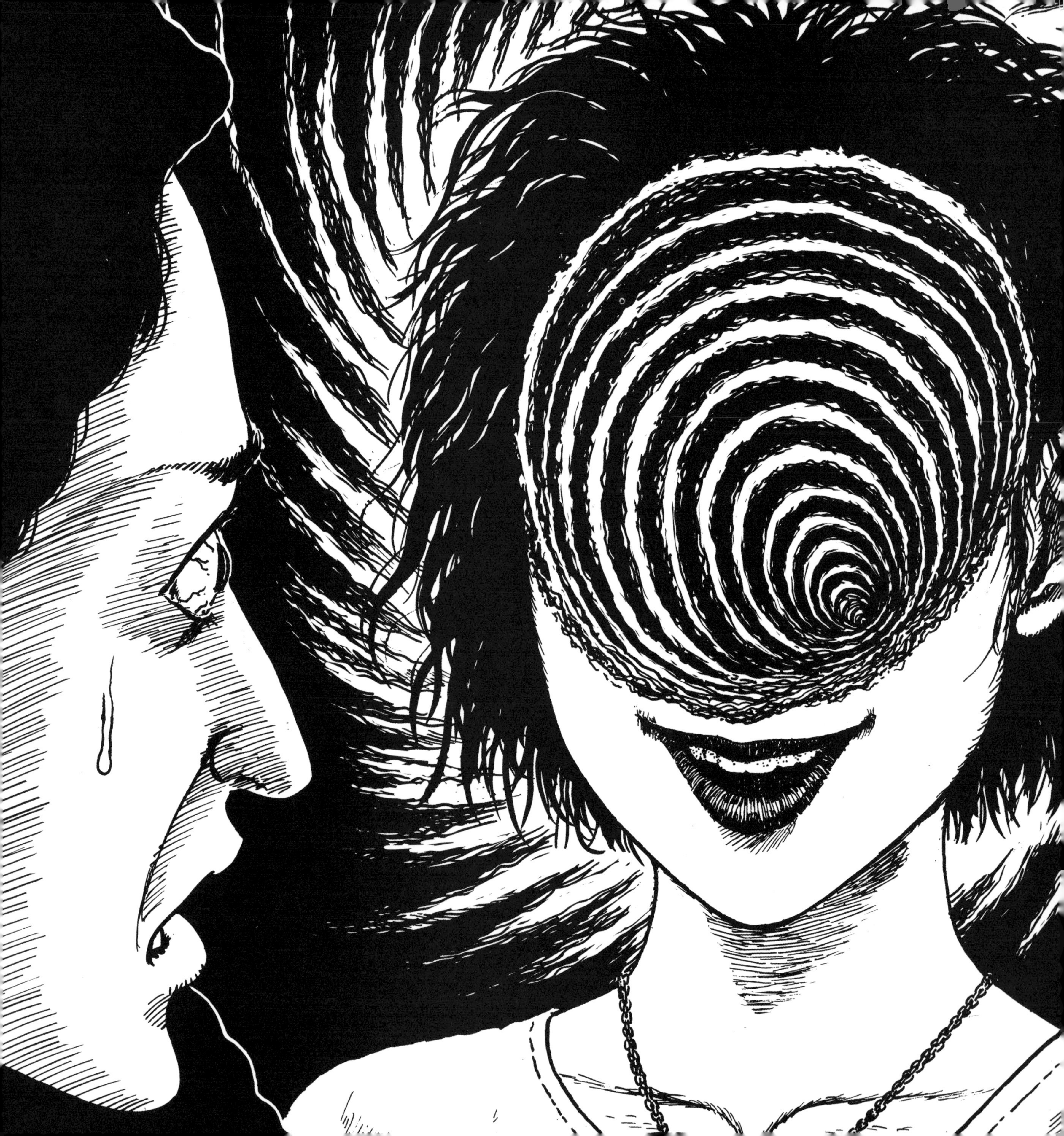

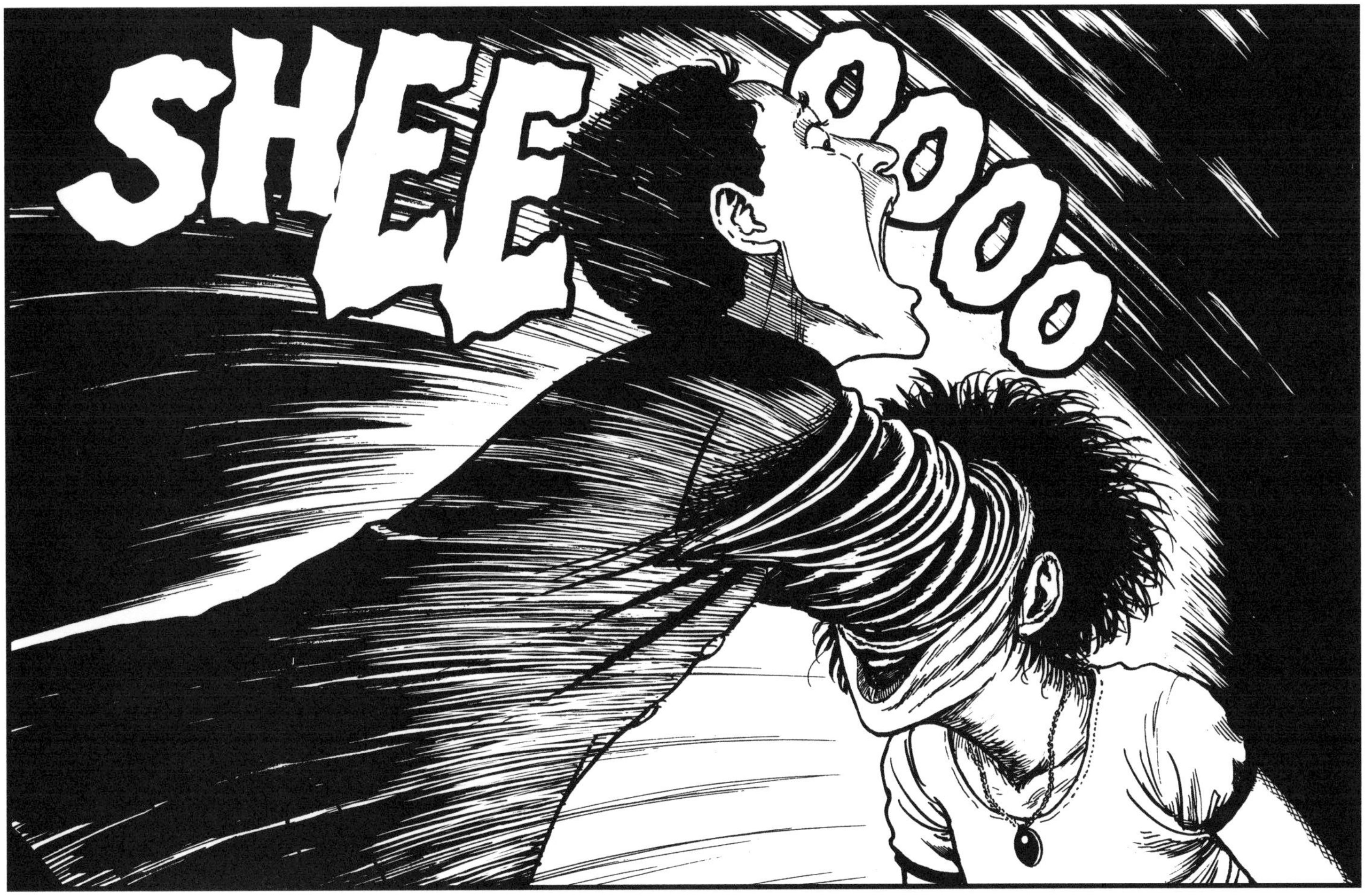
SHEEOOOO

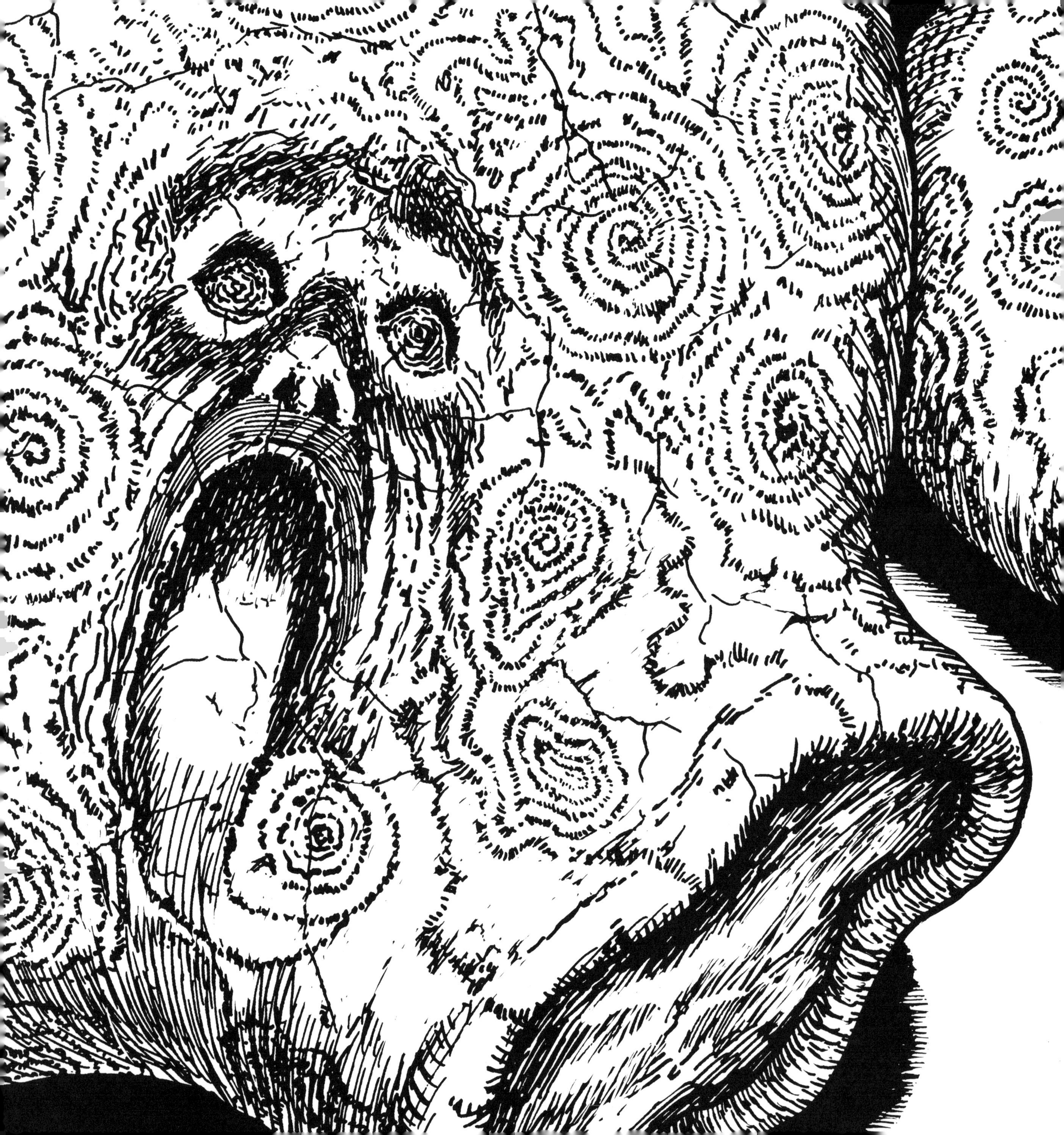

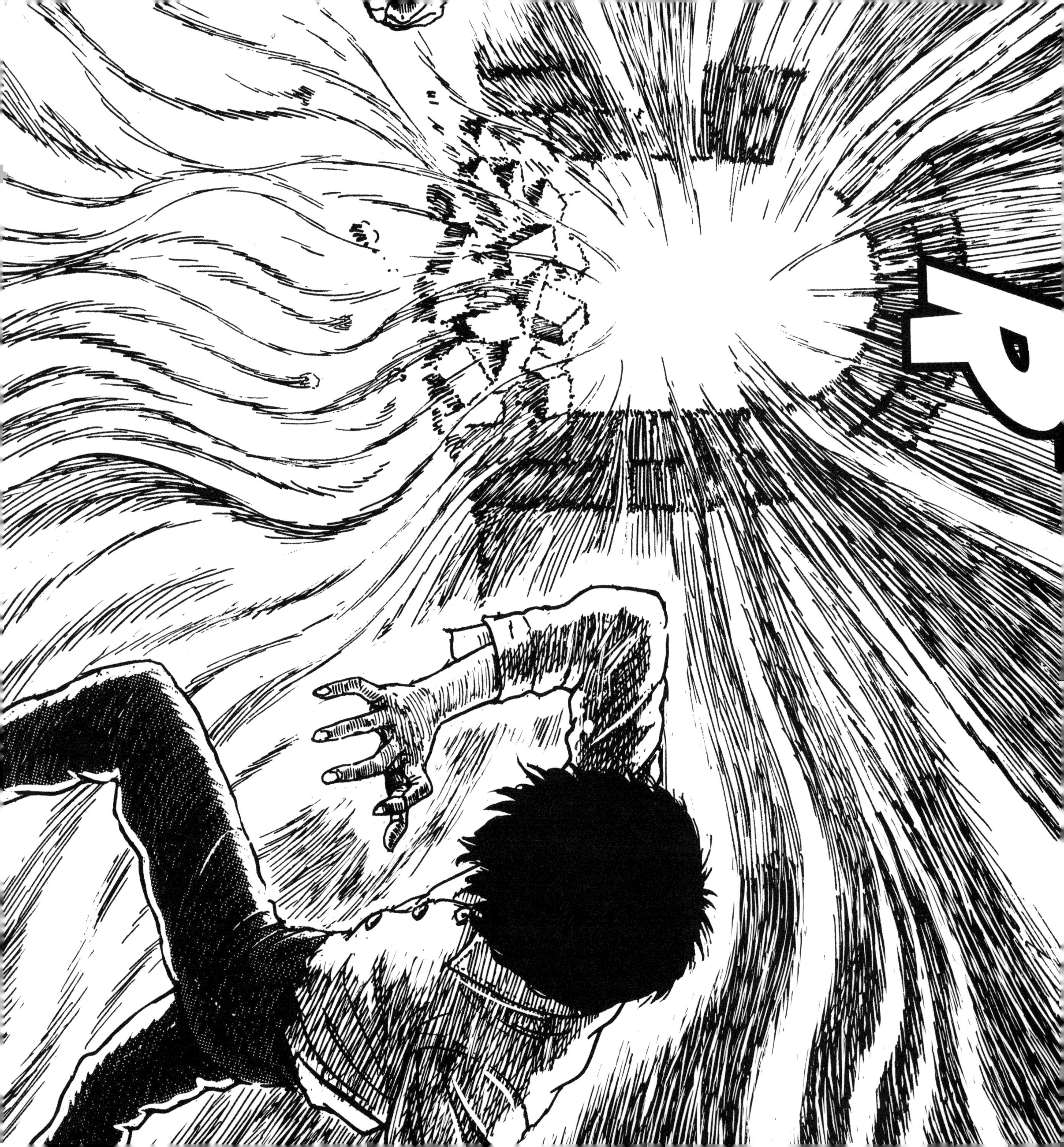

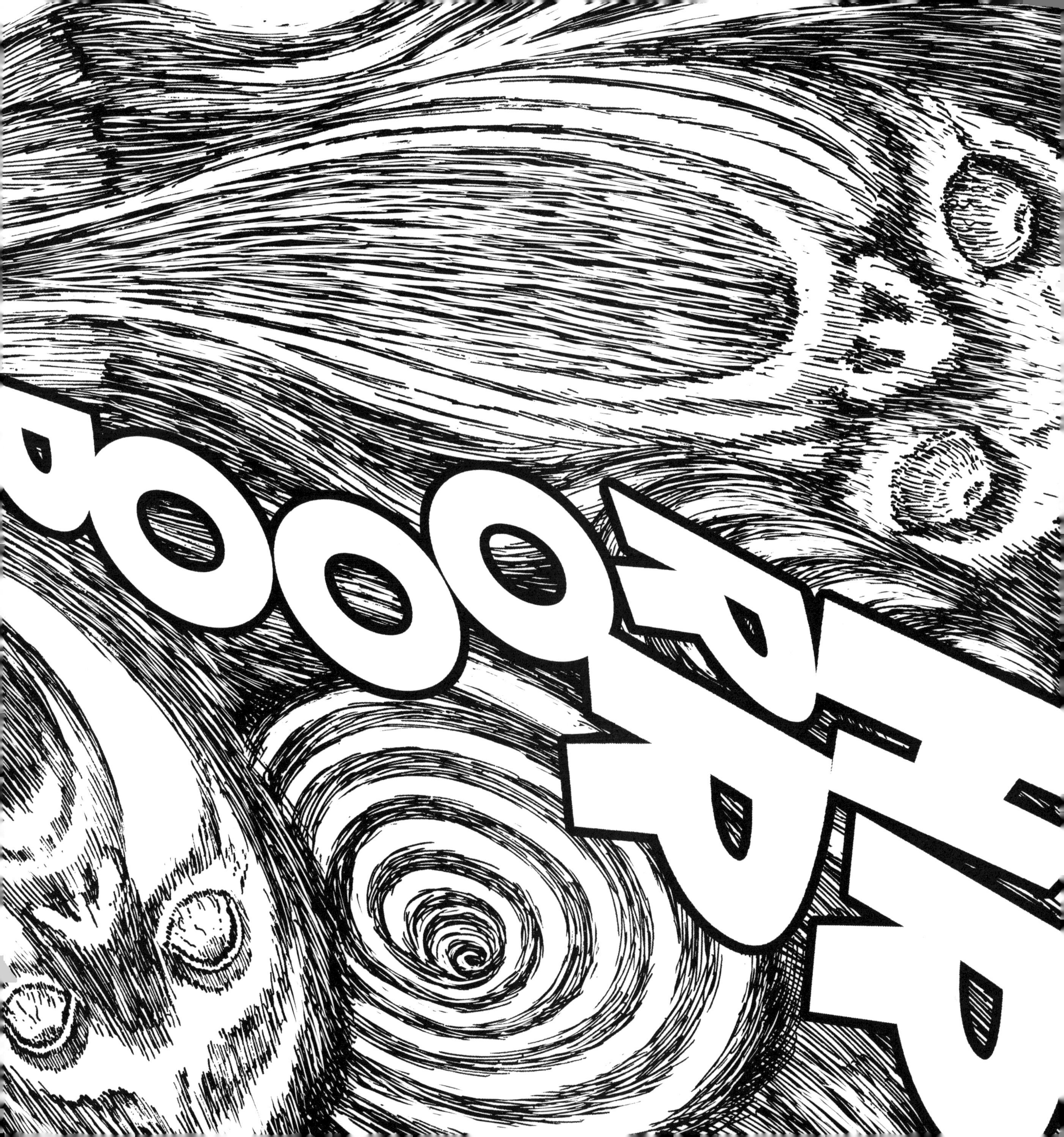

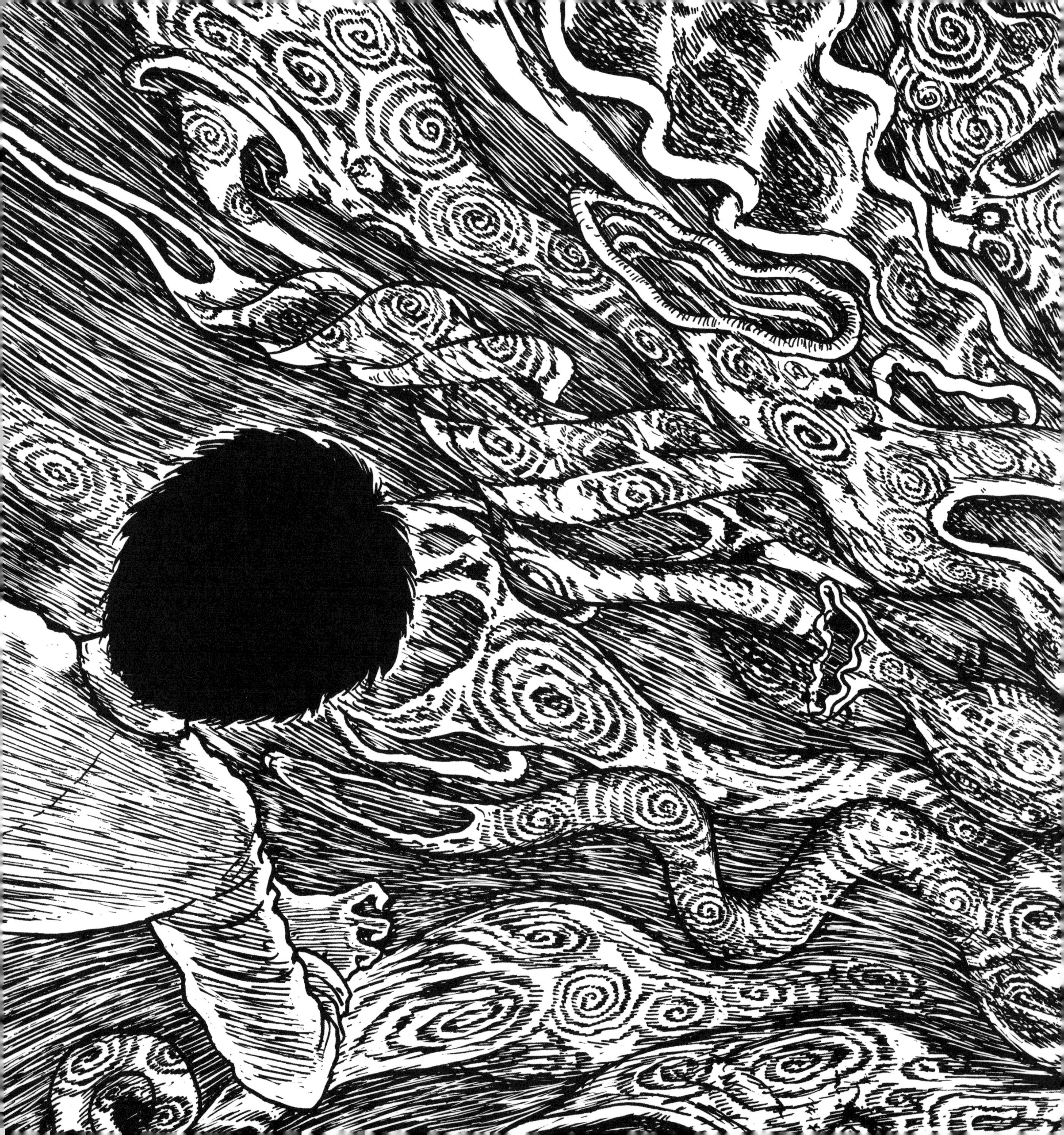

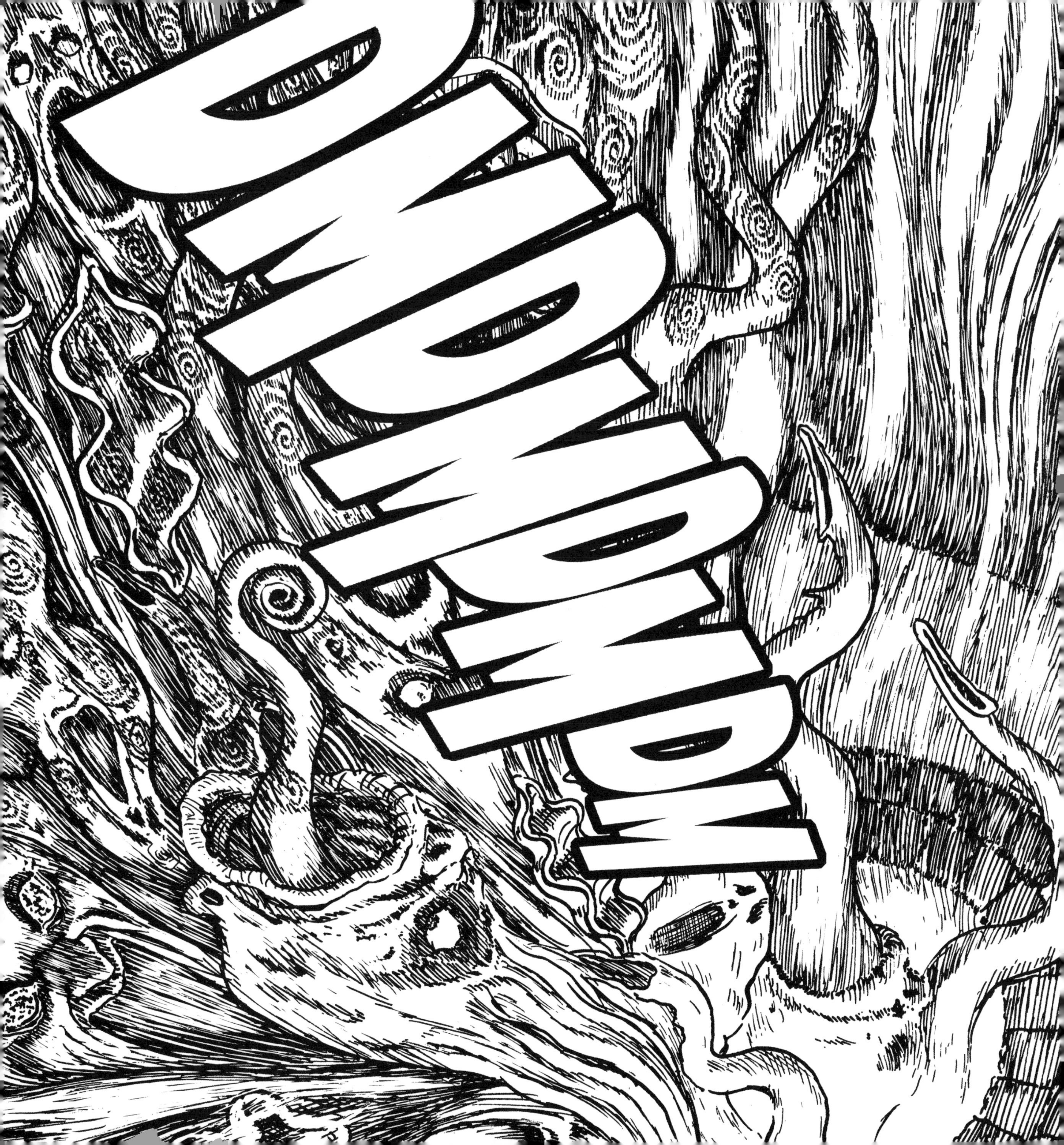
DMDMDMDM

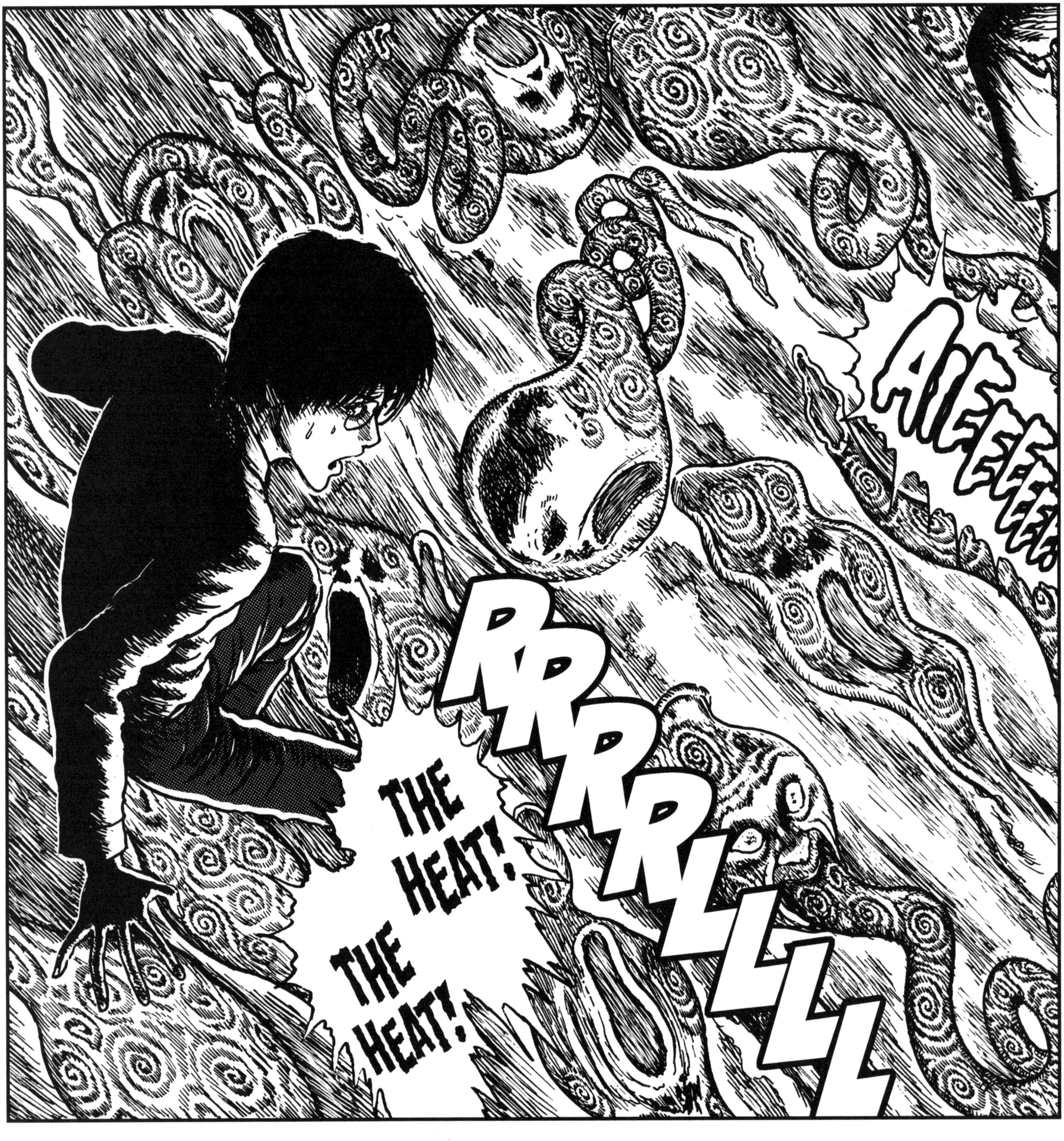
AIEEEEEE
RRRRLLLLL
THE HEAT! THE HEAT!

SHUIIICHIIII!!
TUMP
TUMP
SS
ZZ
SS
ZZ

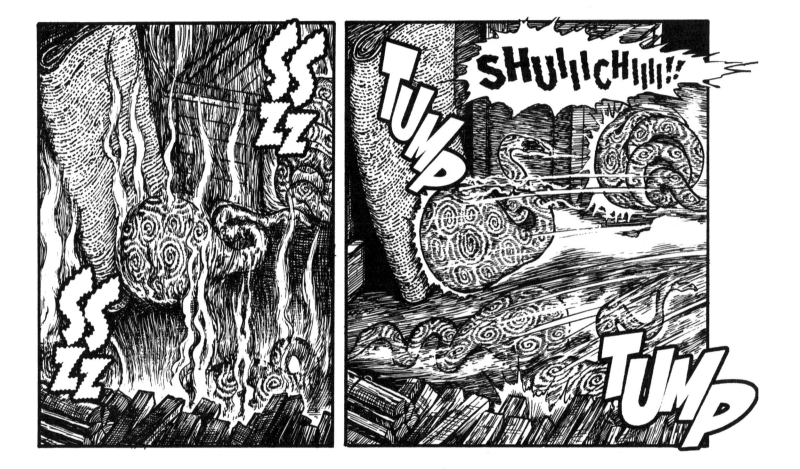

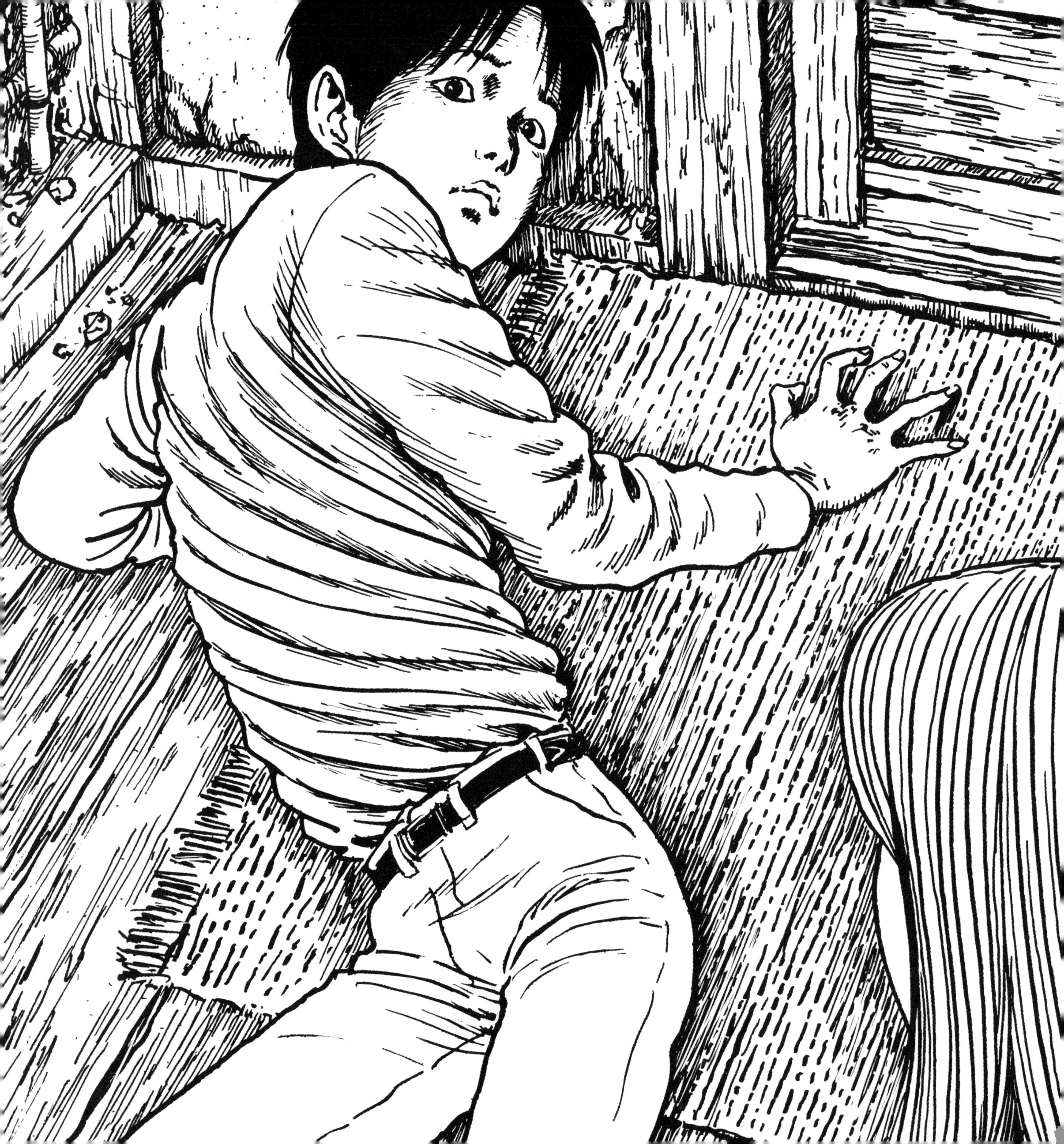

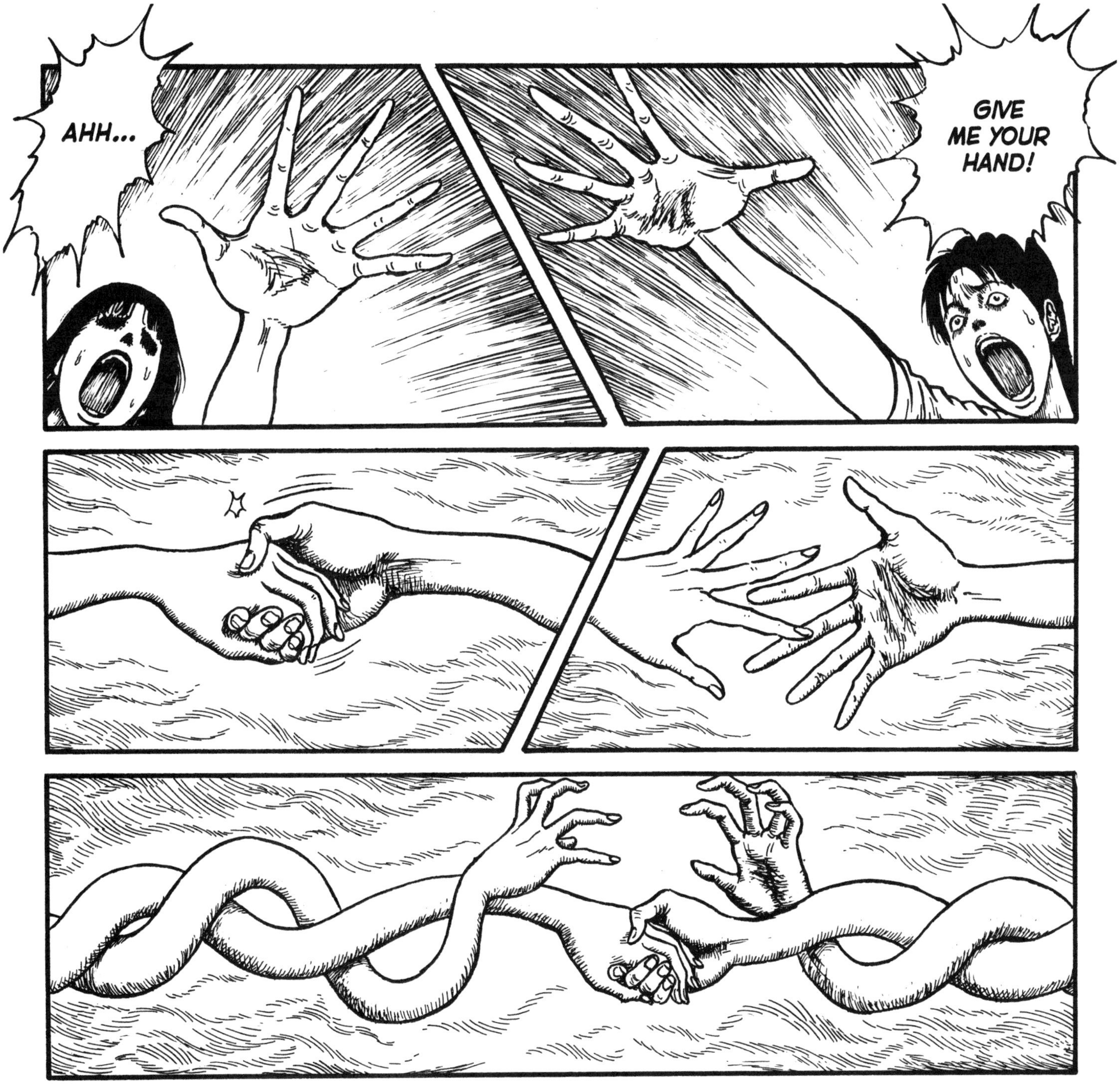
GIVE ME YOUR HAND!
AHH...

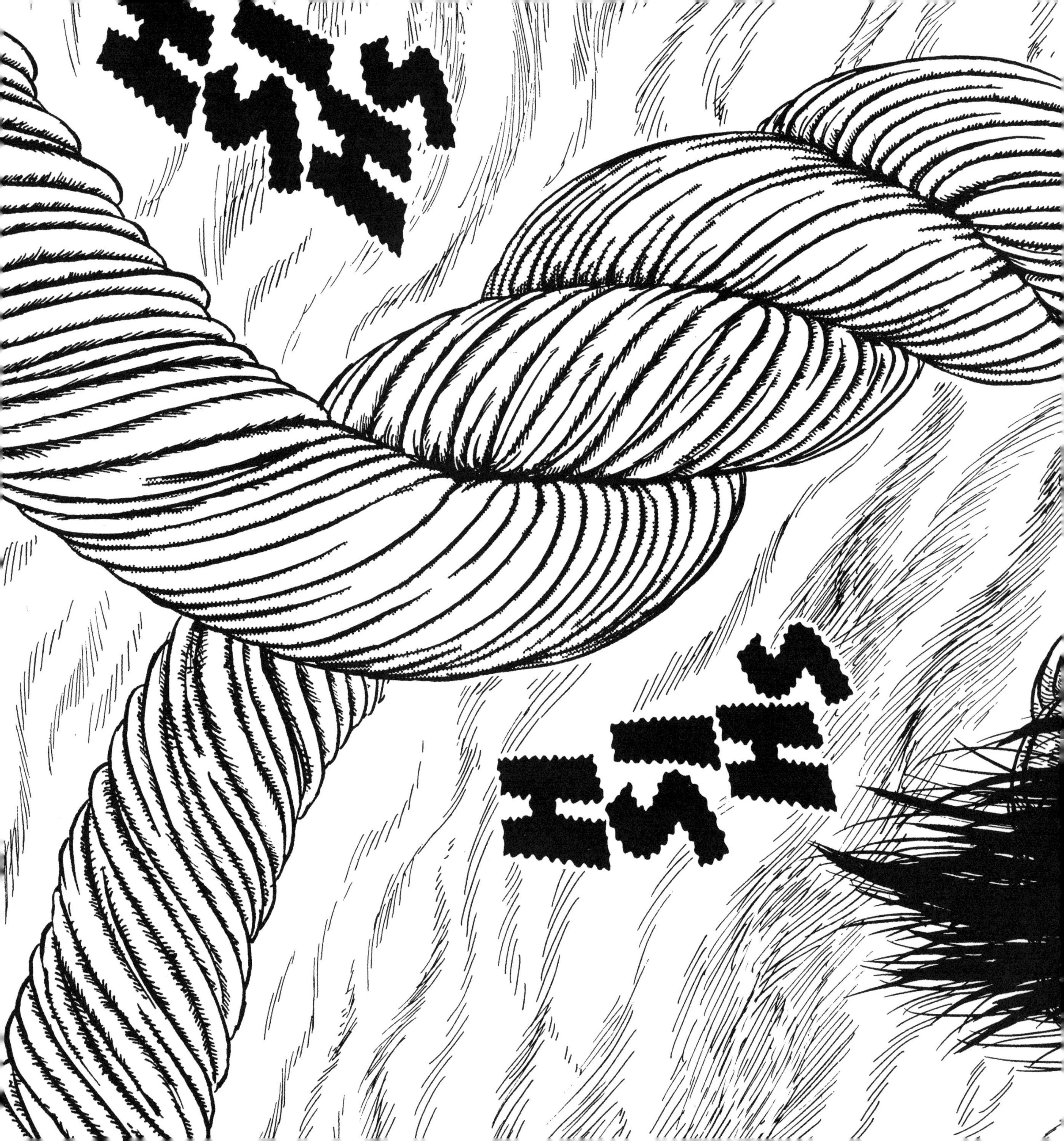

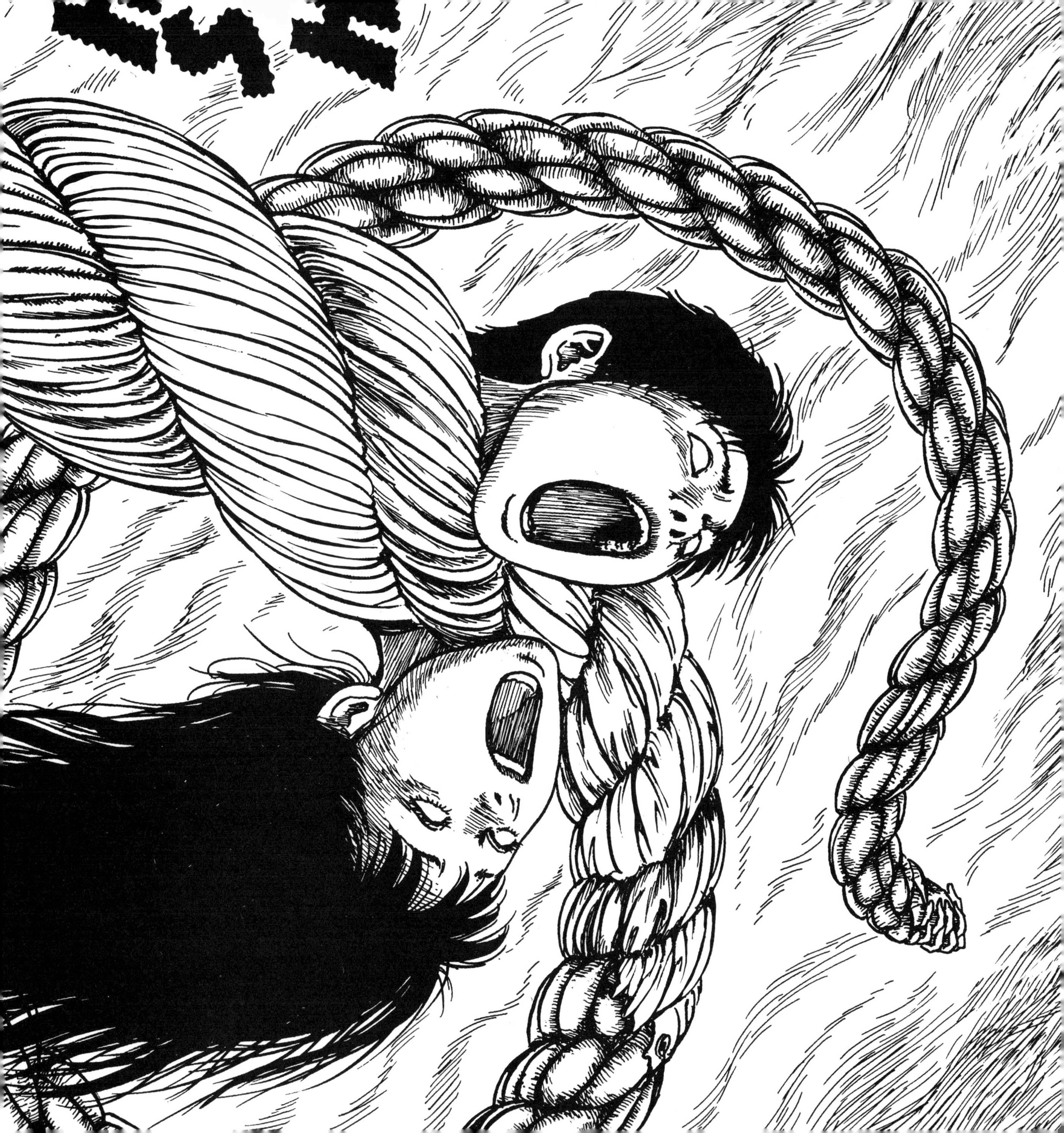

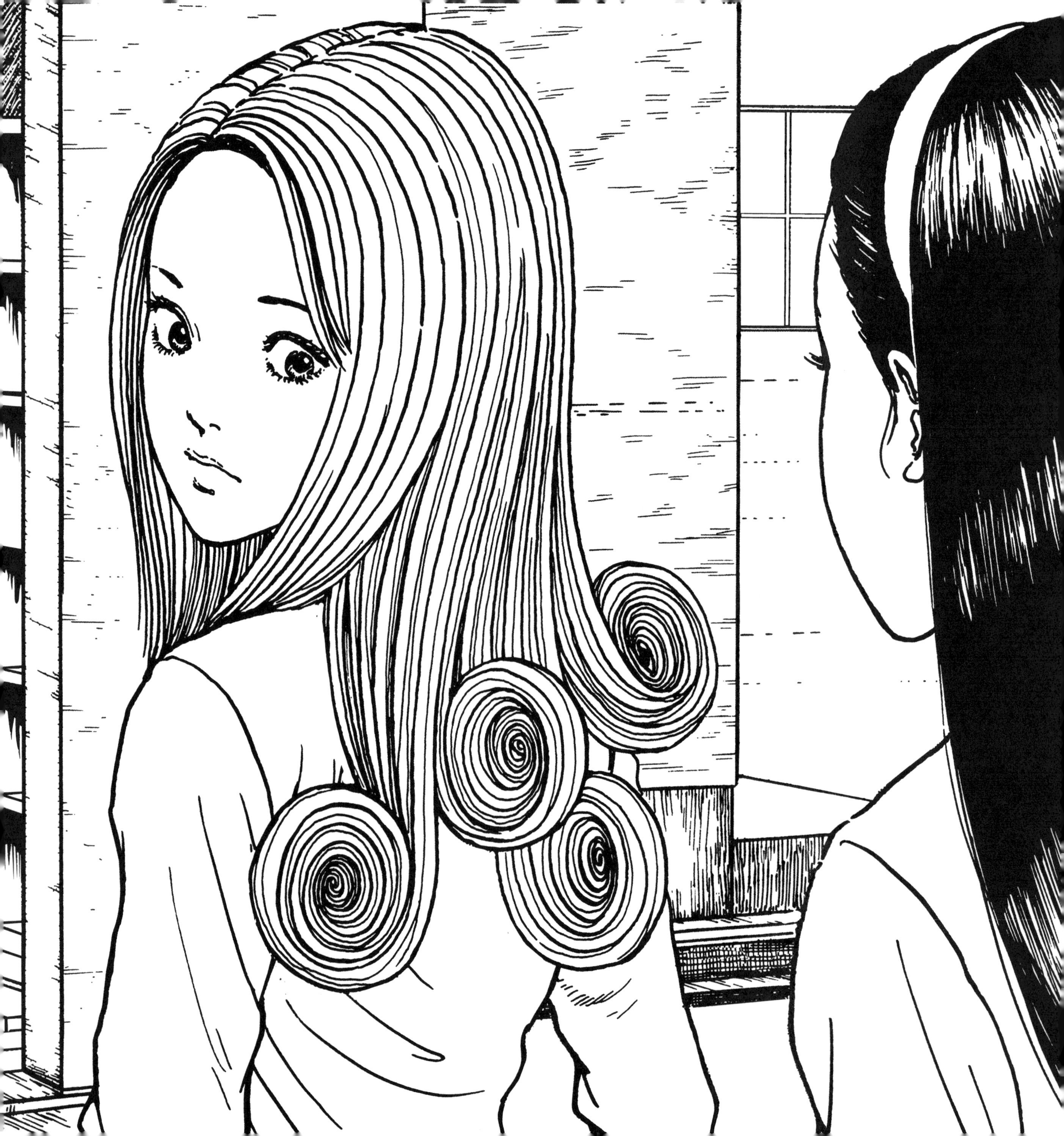

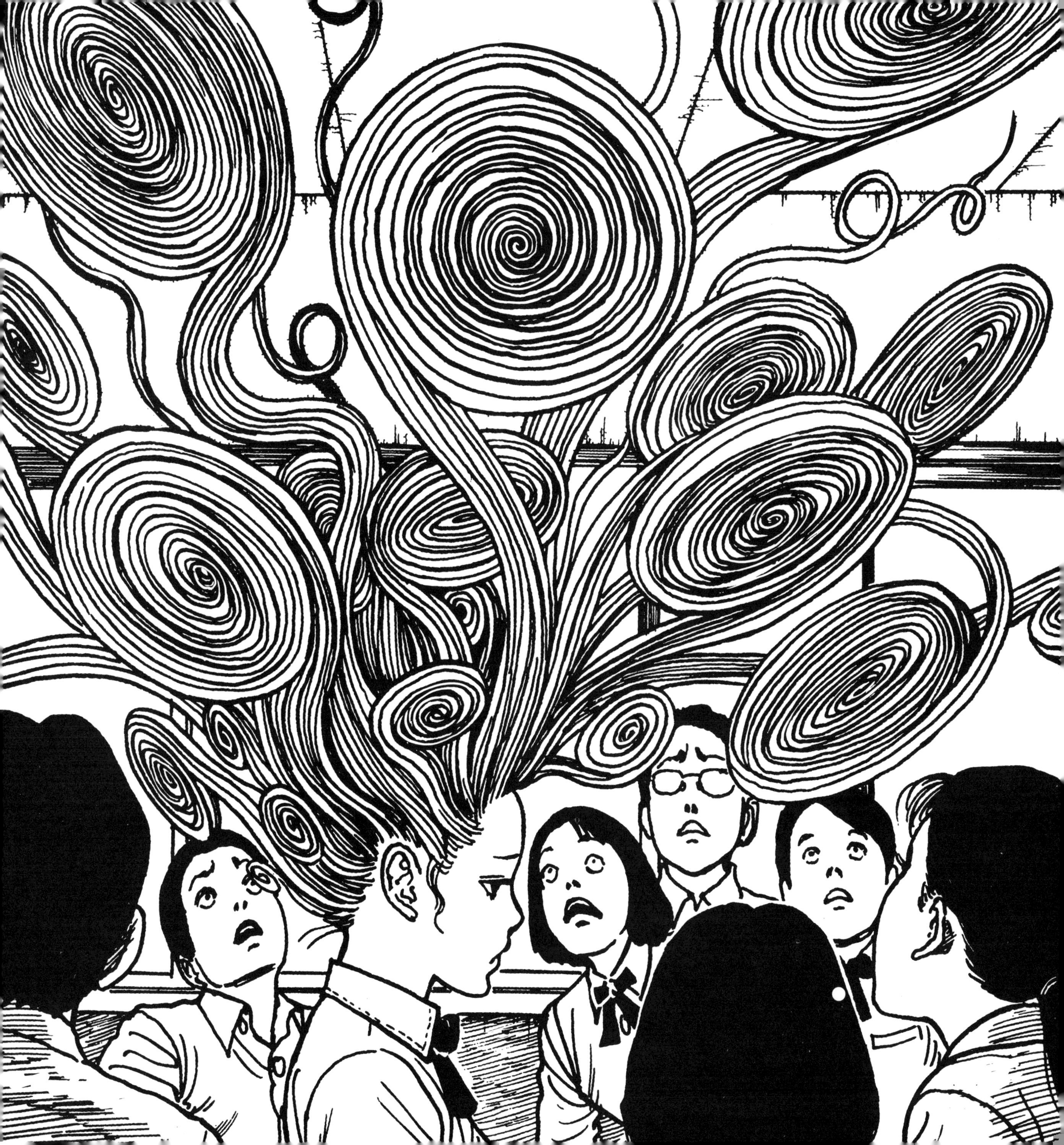

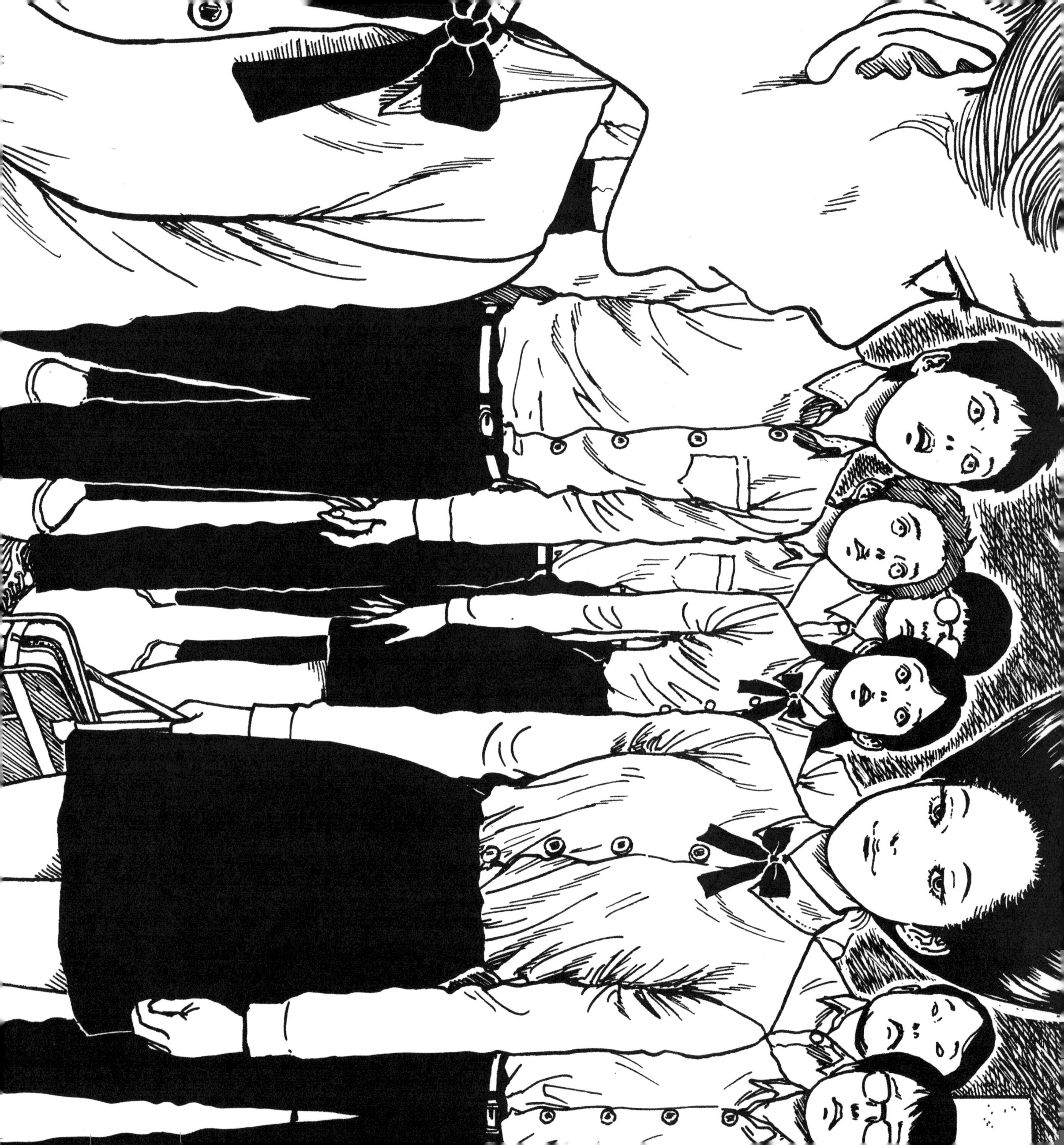

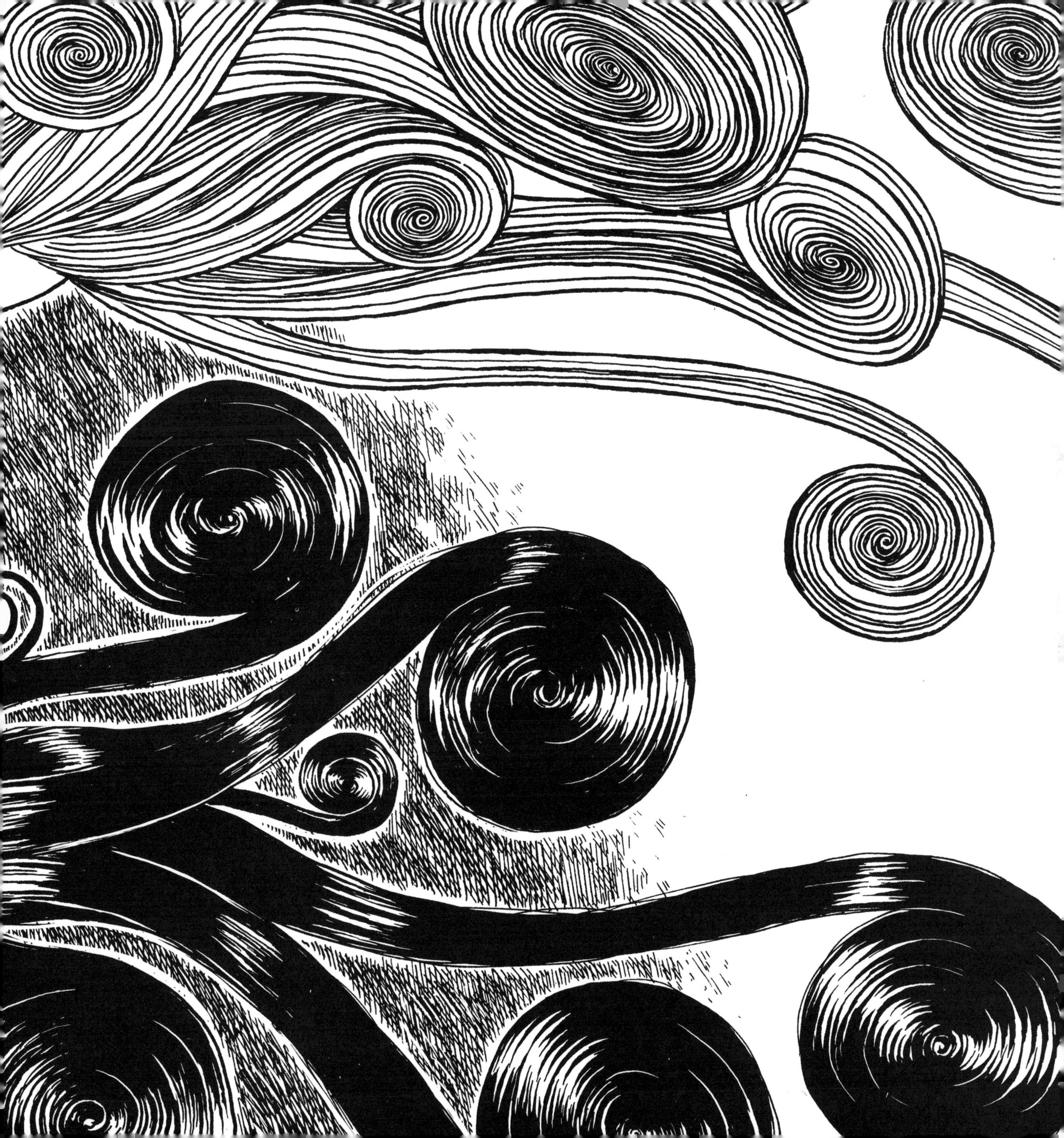

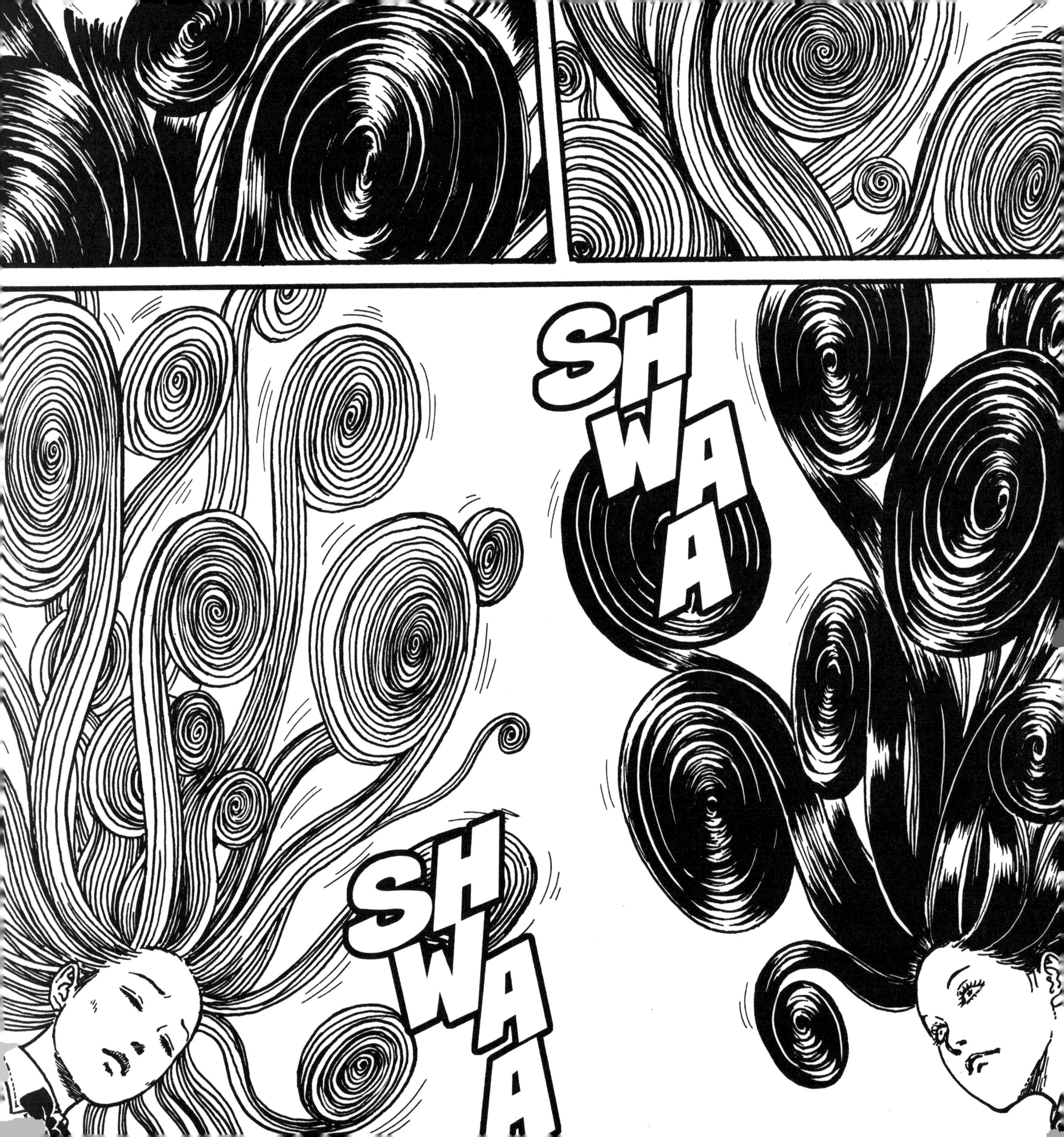
SHWAA
SHWAAA

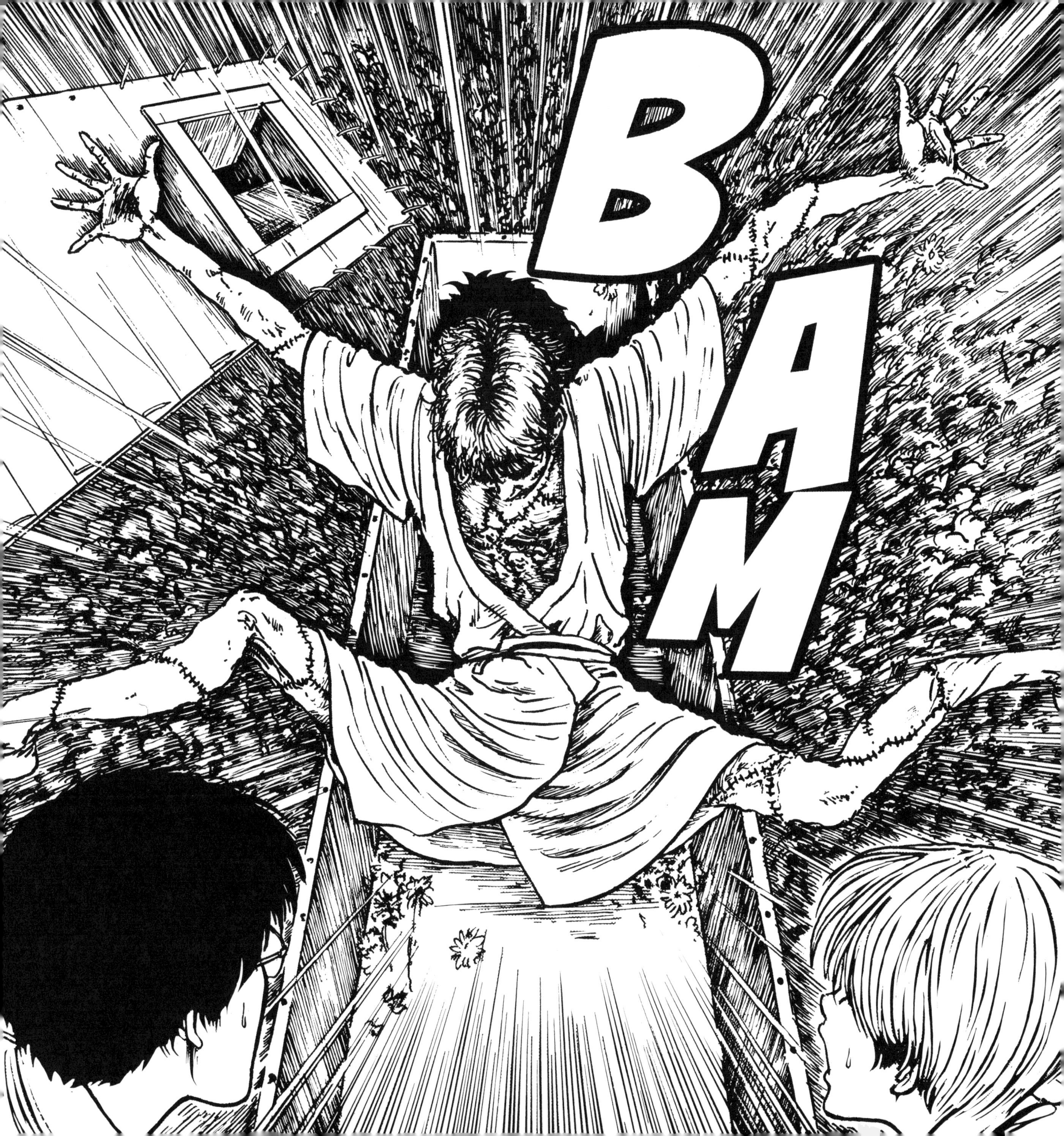
BAM

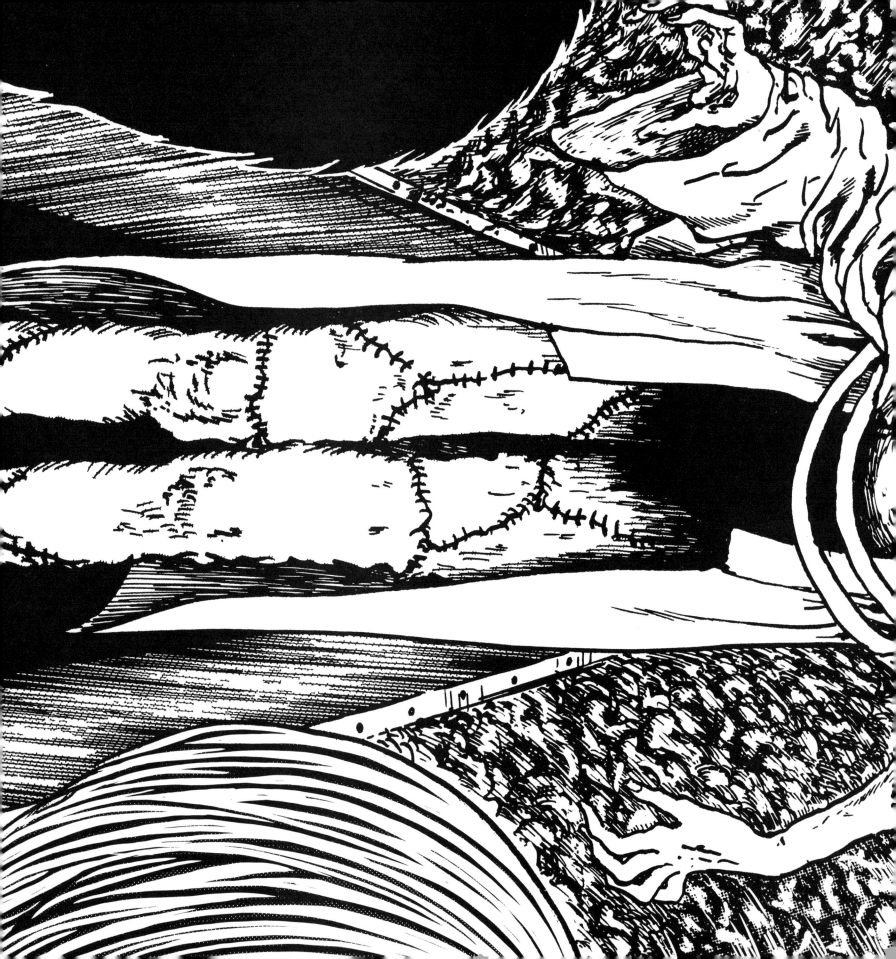

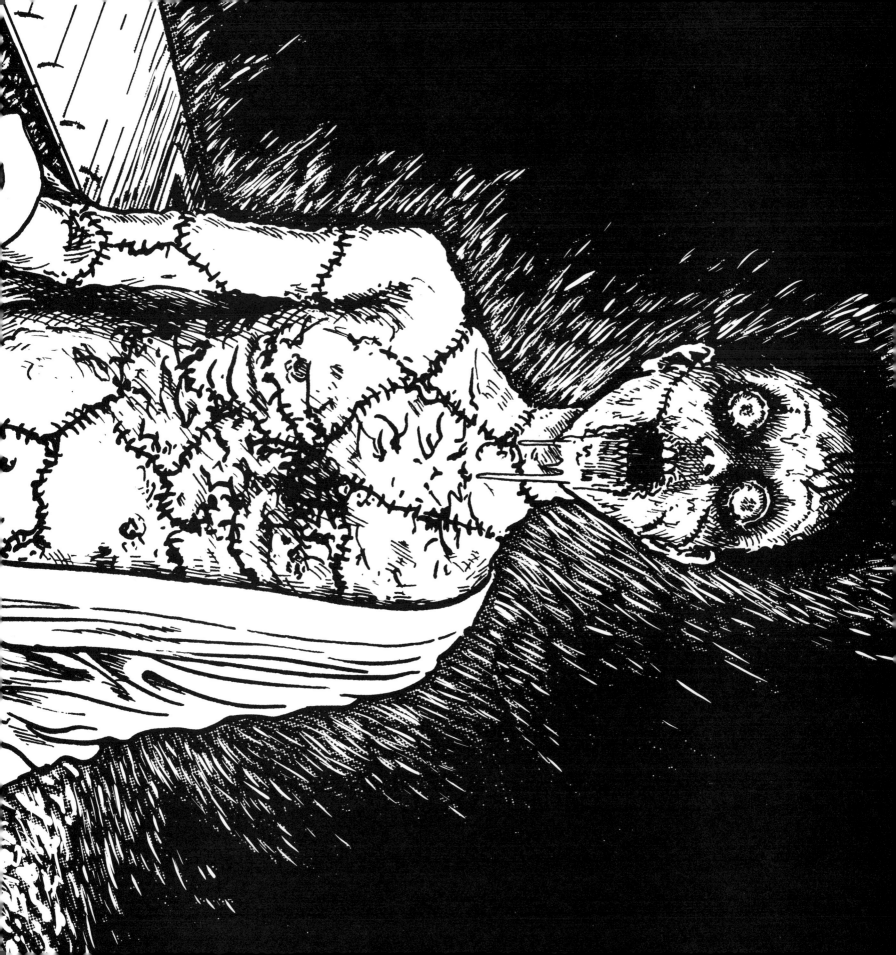

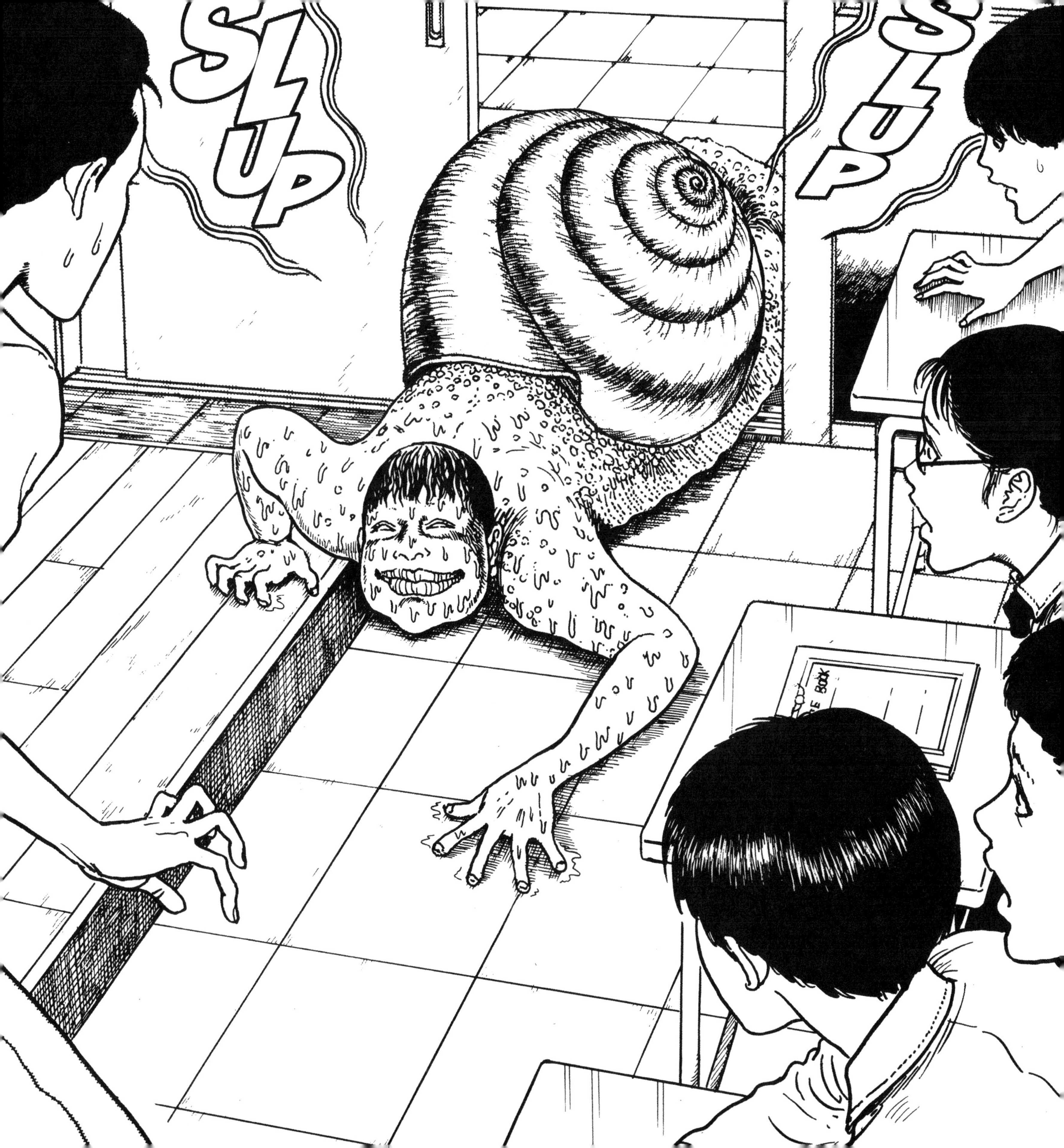
SLUP
SLUP

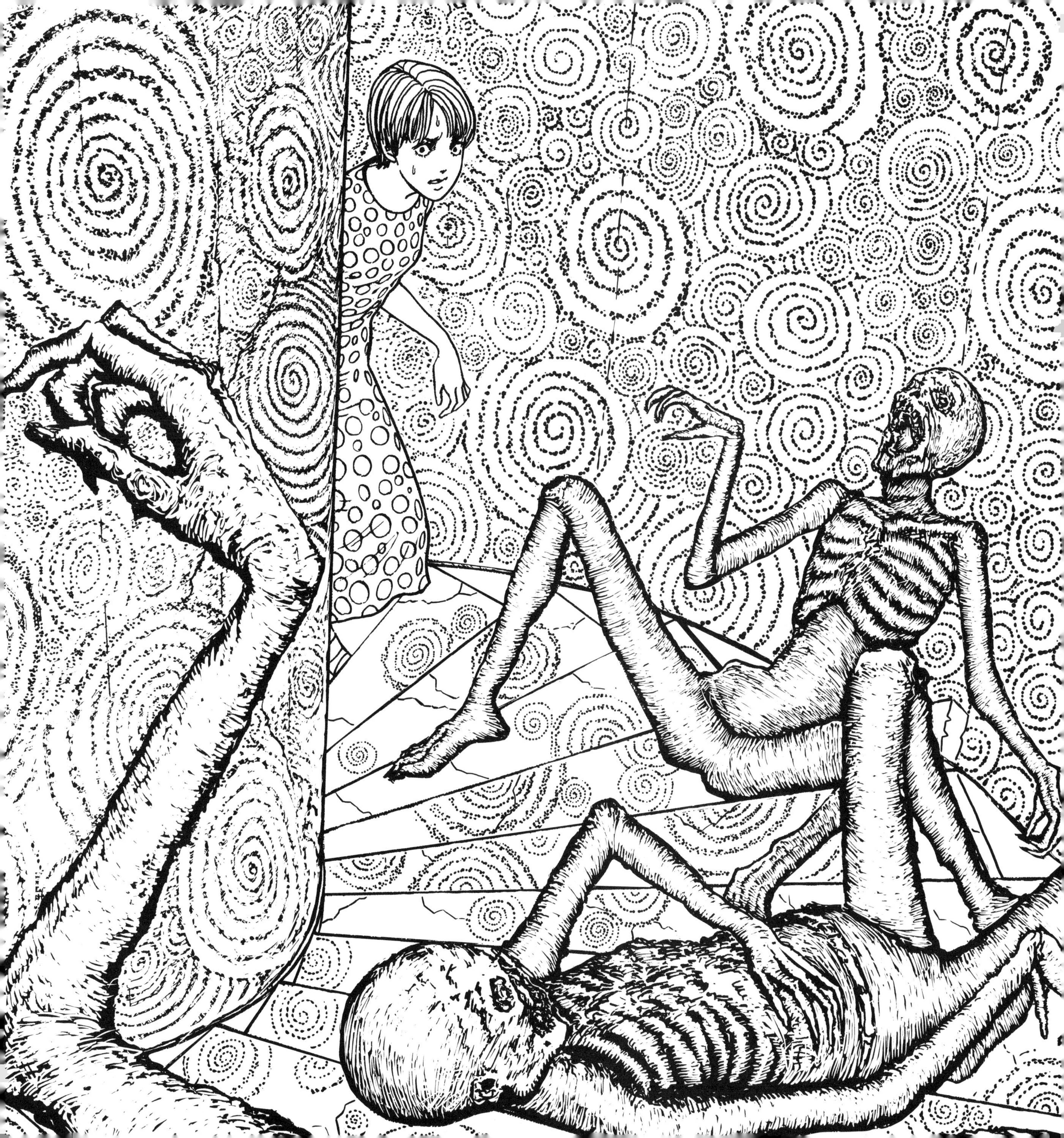

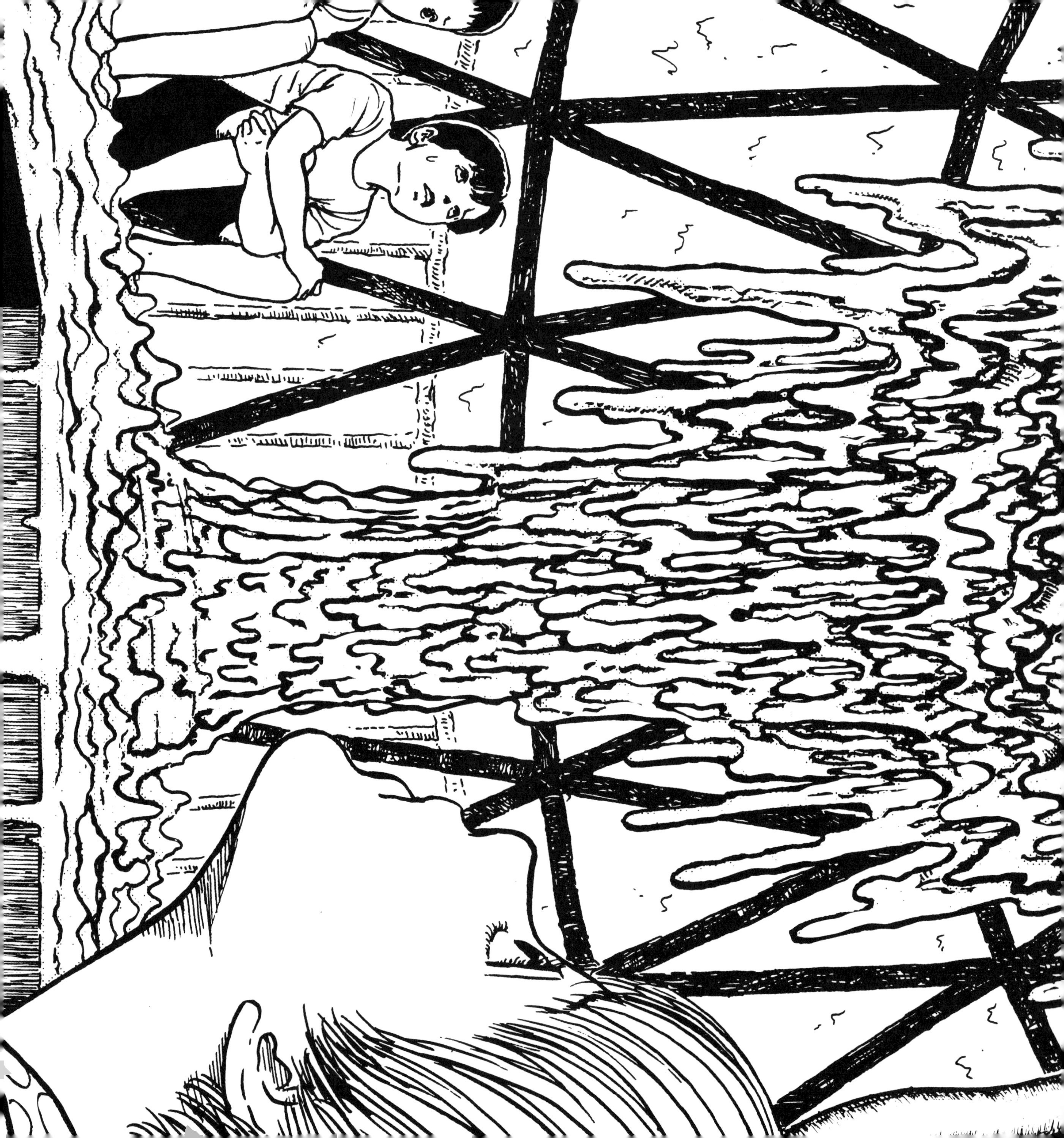

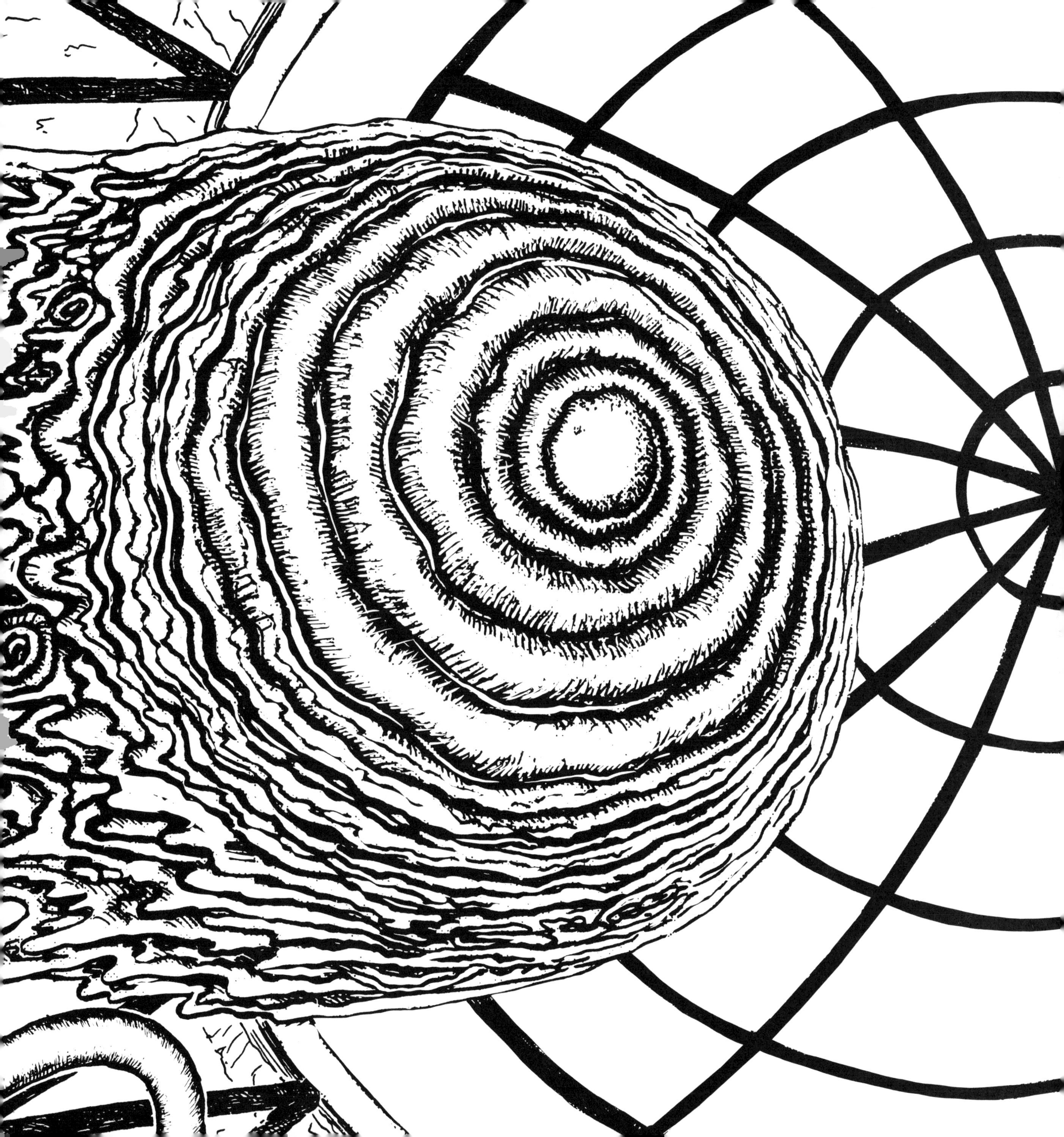

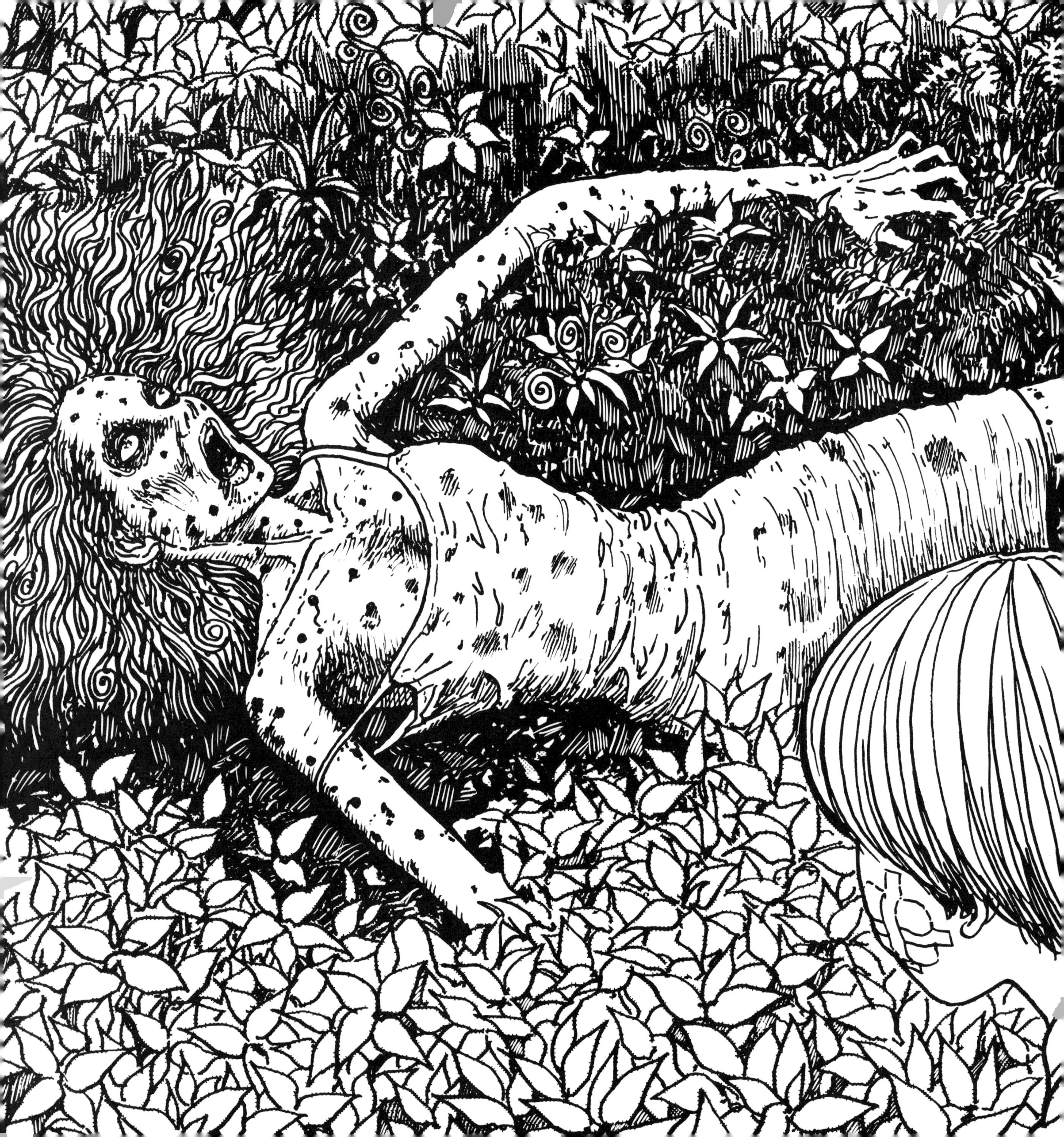

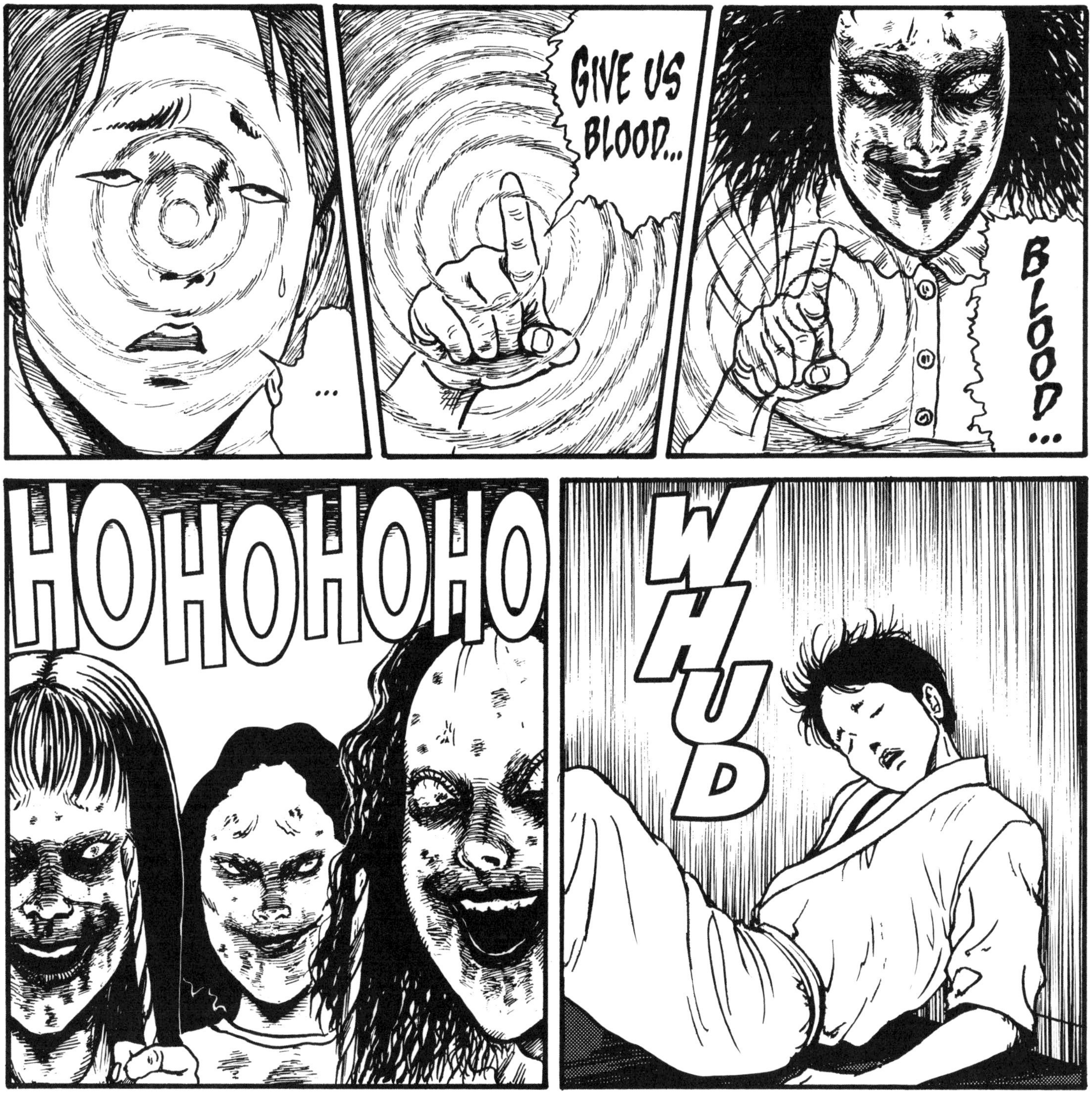
...
GIVE US BLOOD...
BLOOD...
HOHOHOHOHO
WHUD

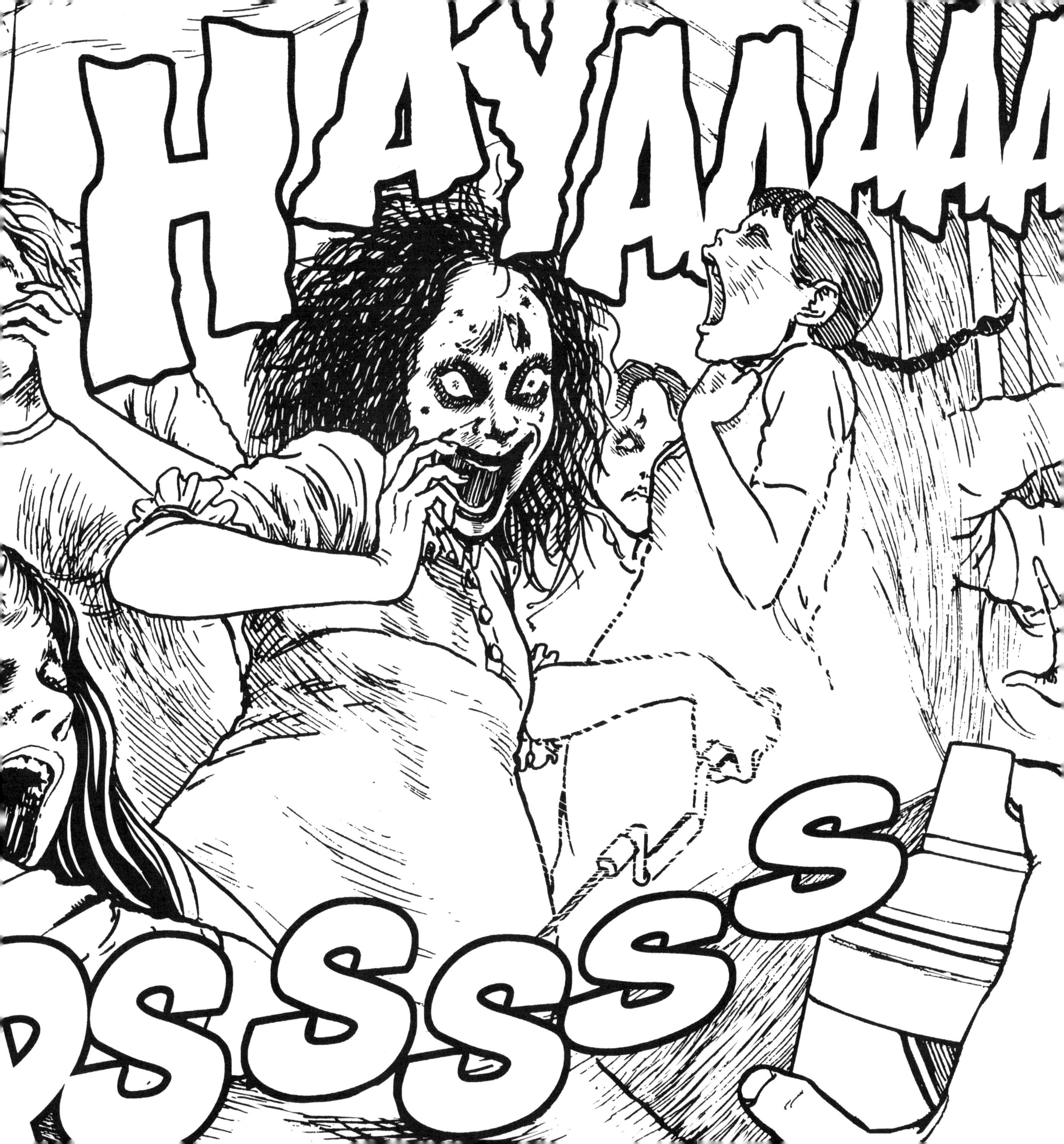
HAYAAAA
SSSSS

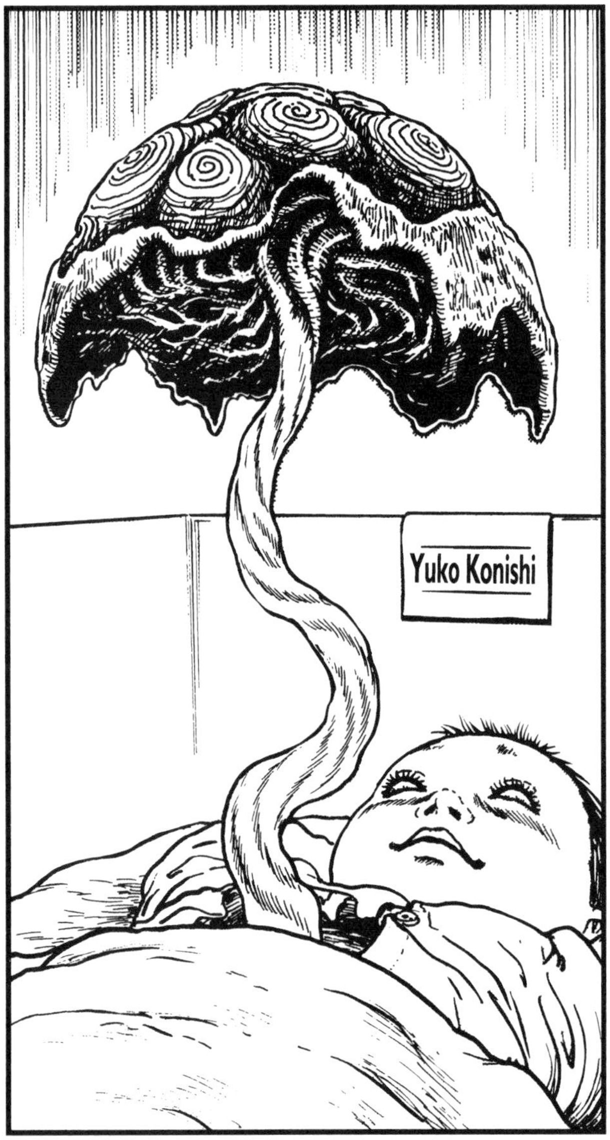
Yuko Konishi

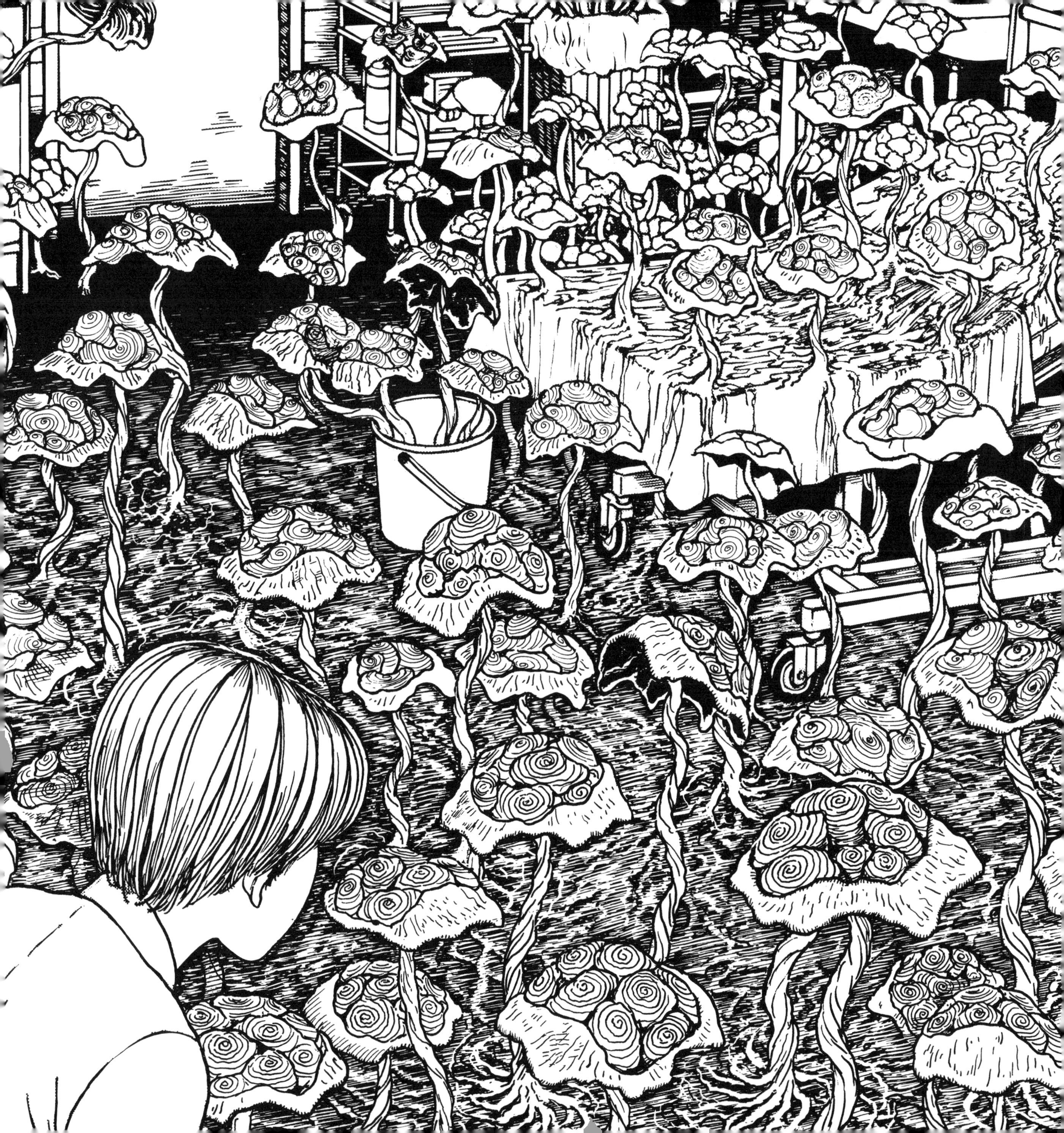

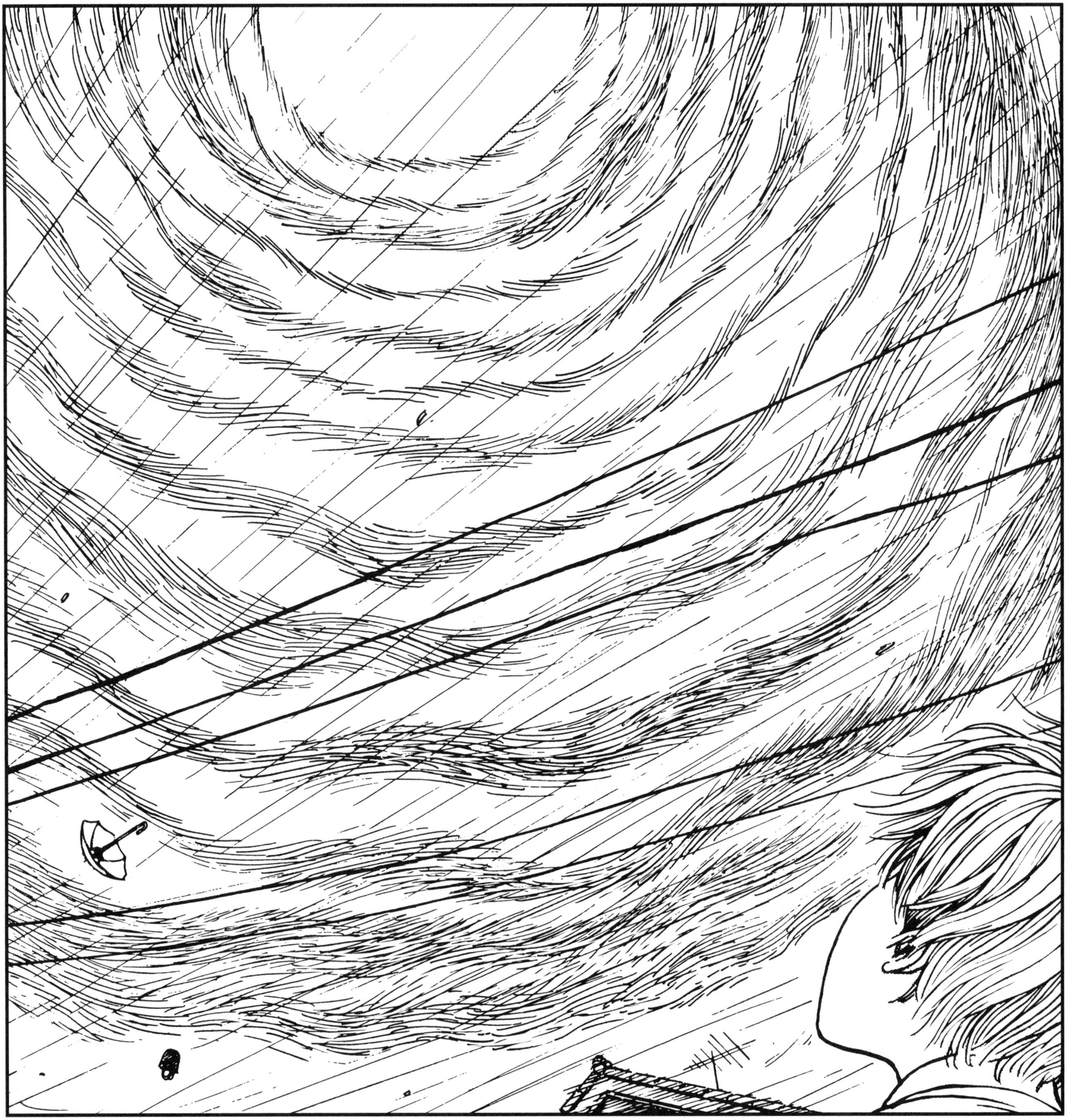

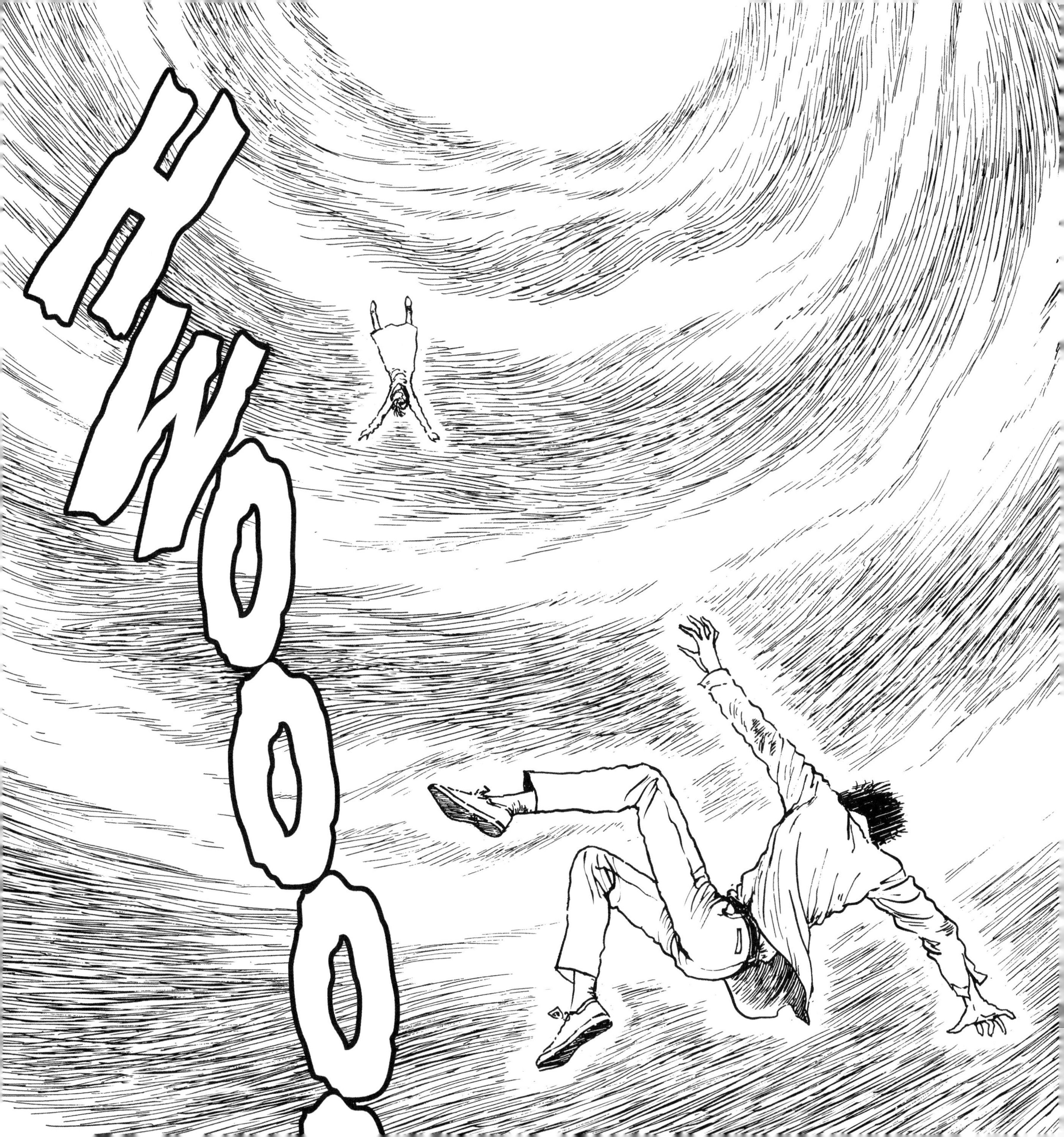
HWOOOO

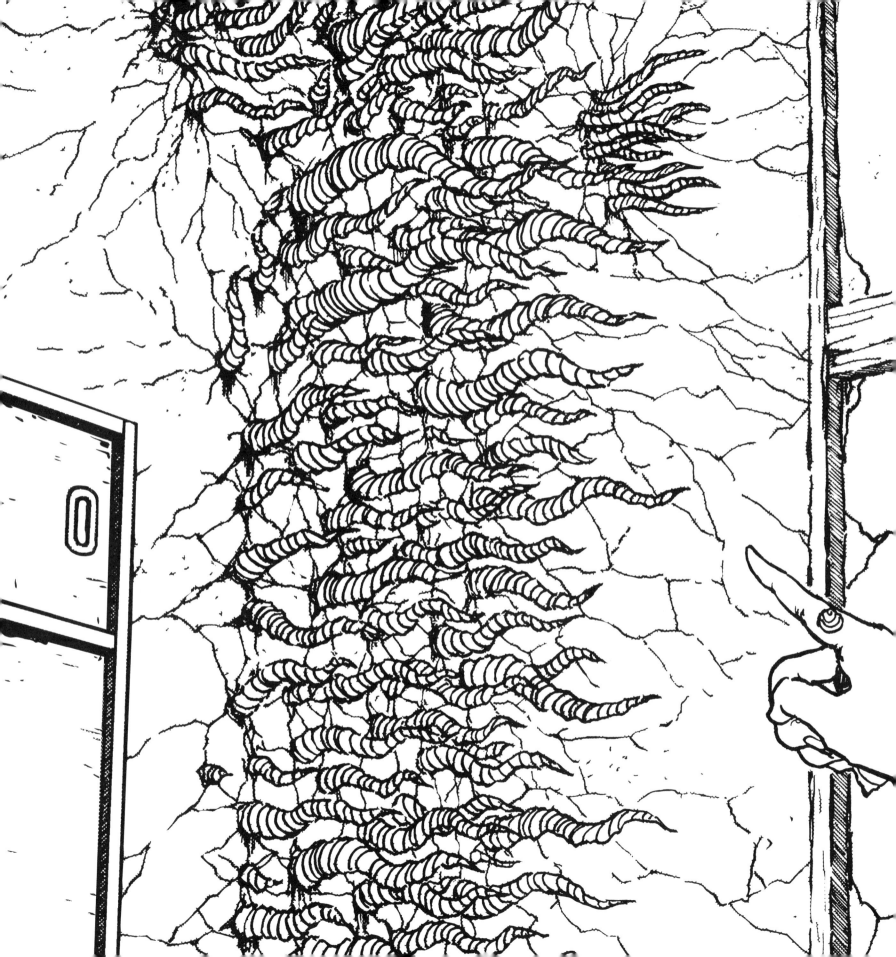

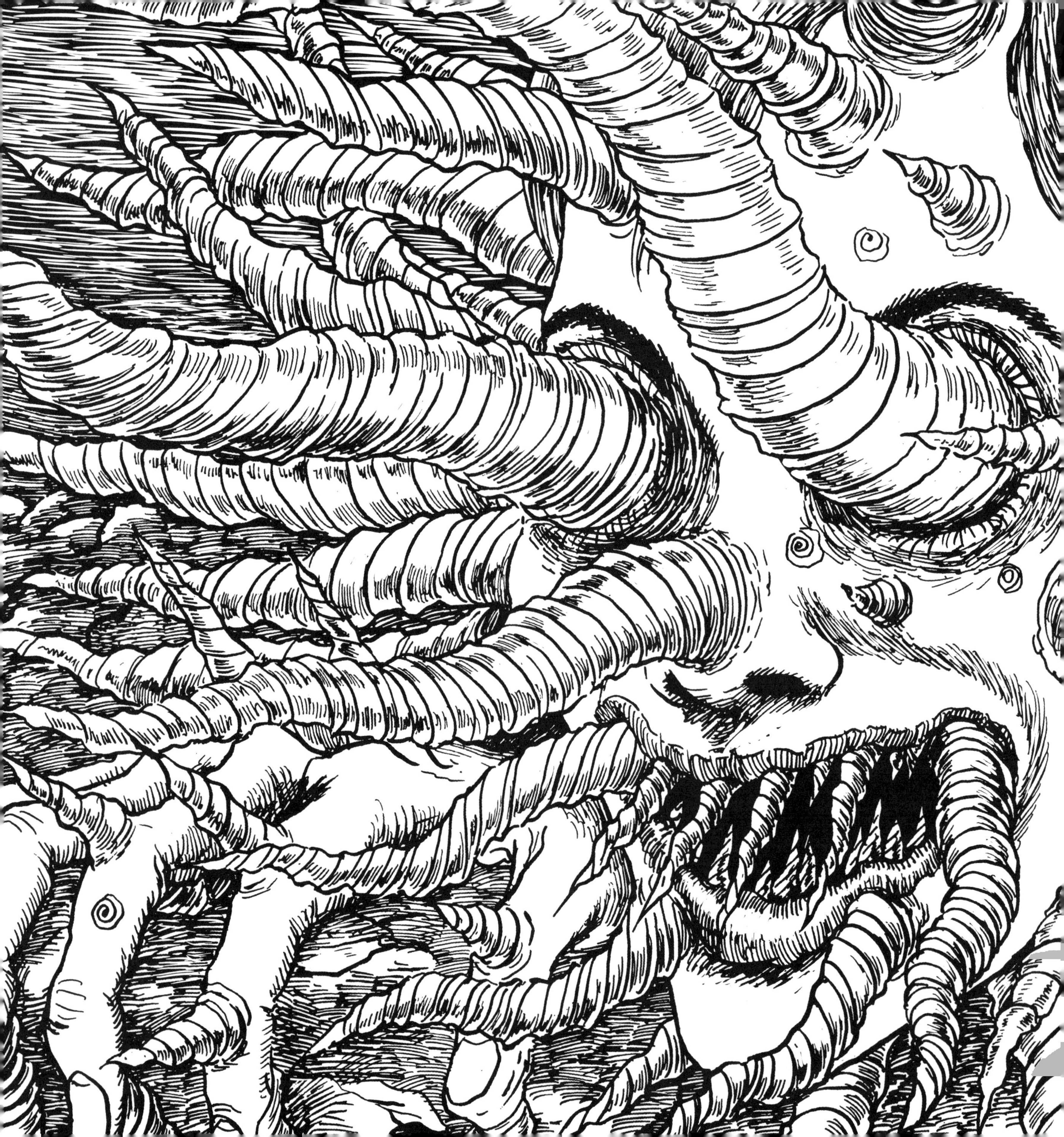

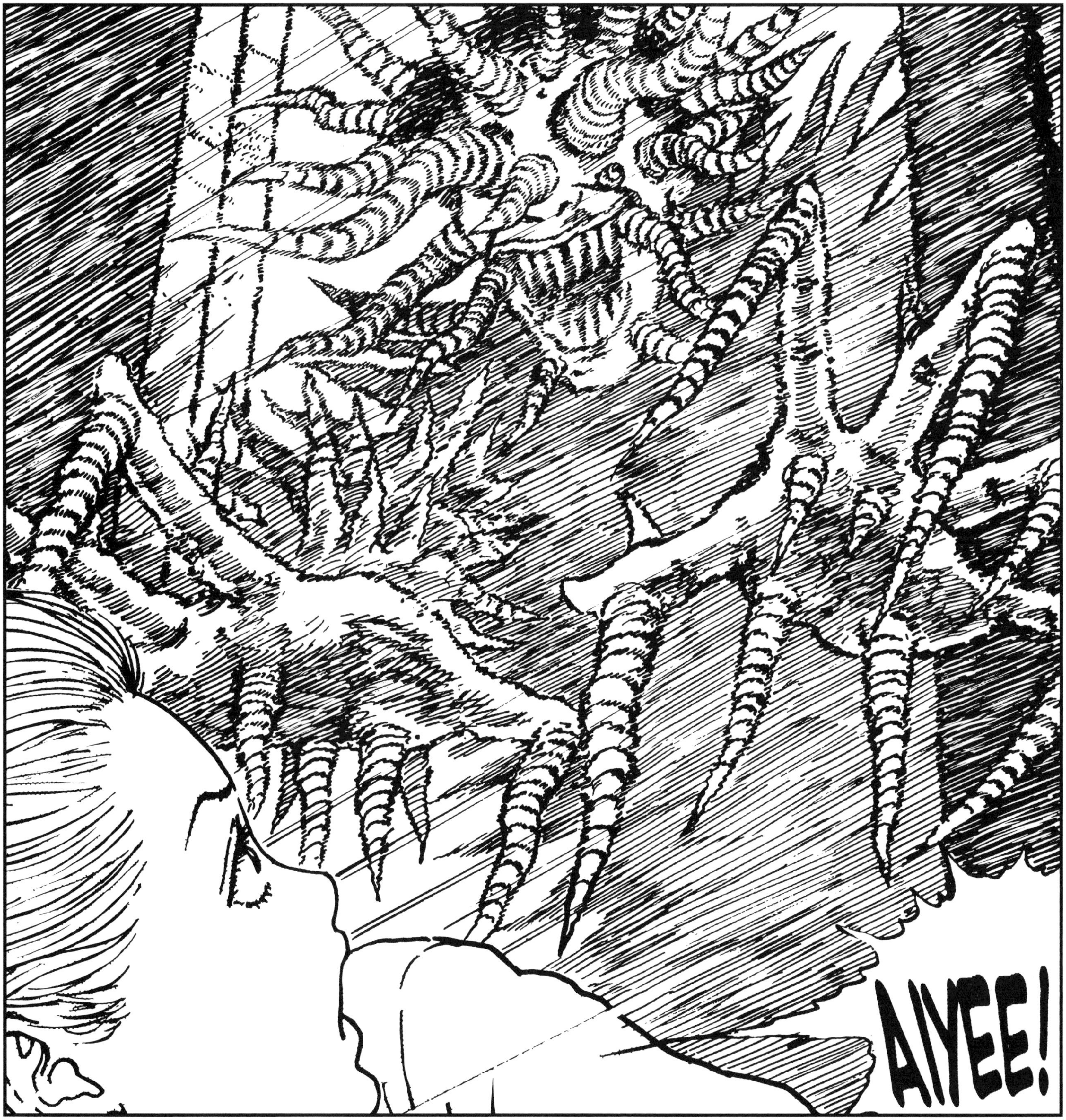
AIYEE!

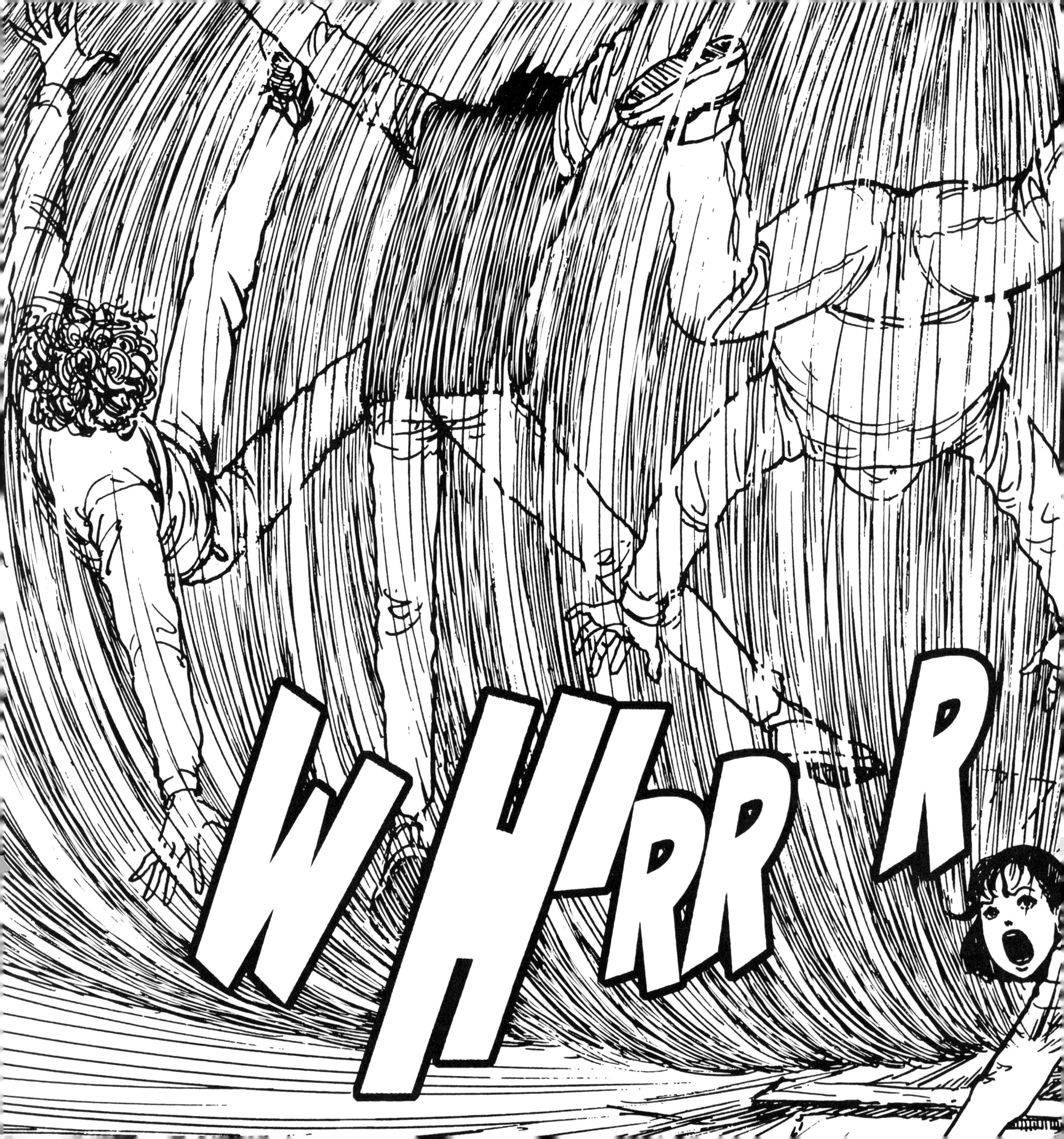
WHIRRR

FWOO!!

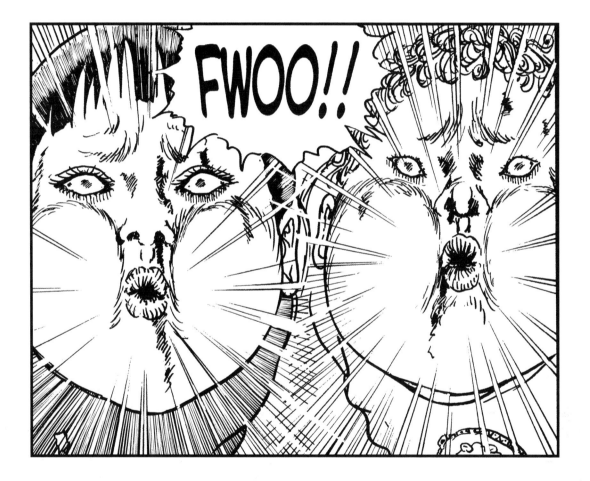

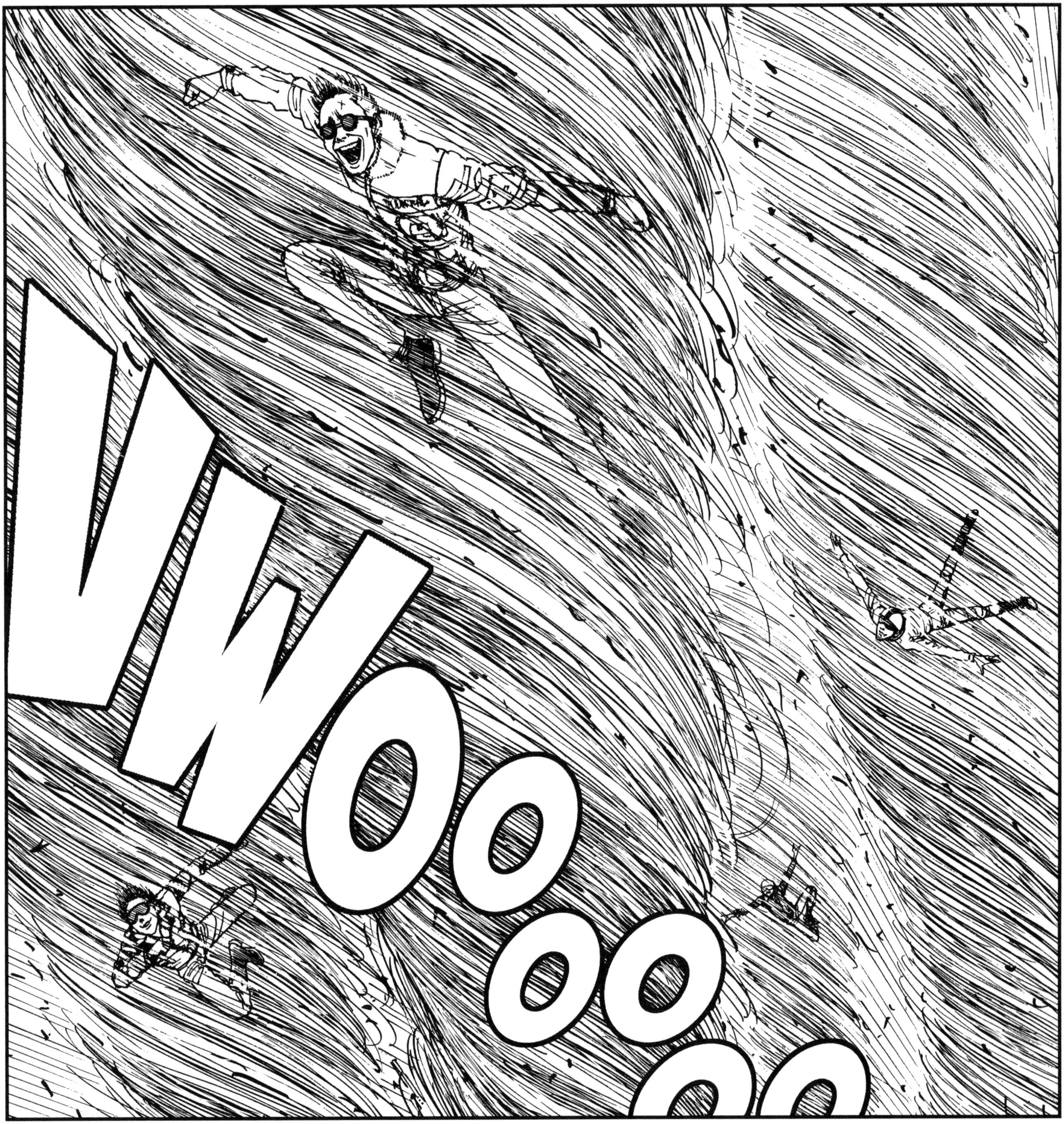
VWOOOOOO

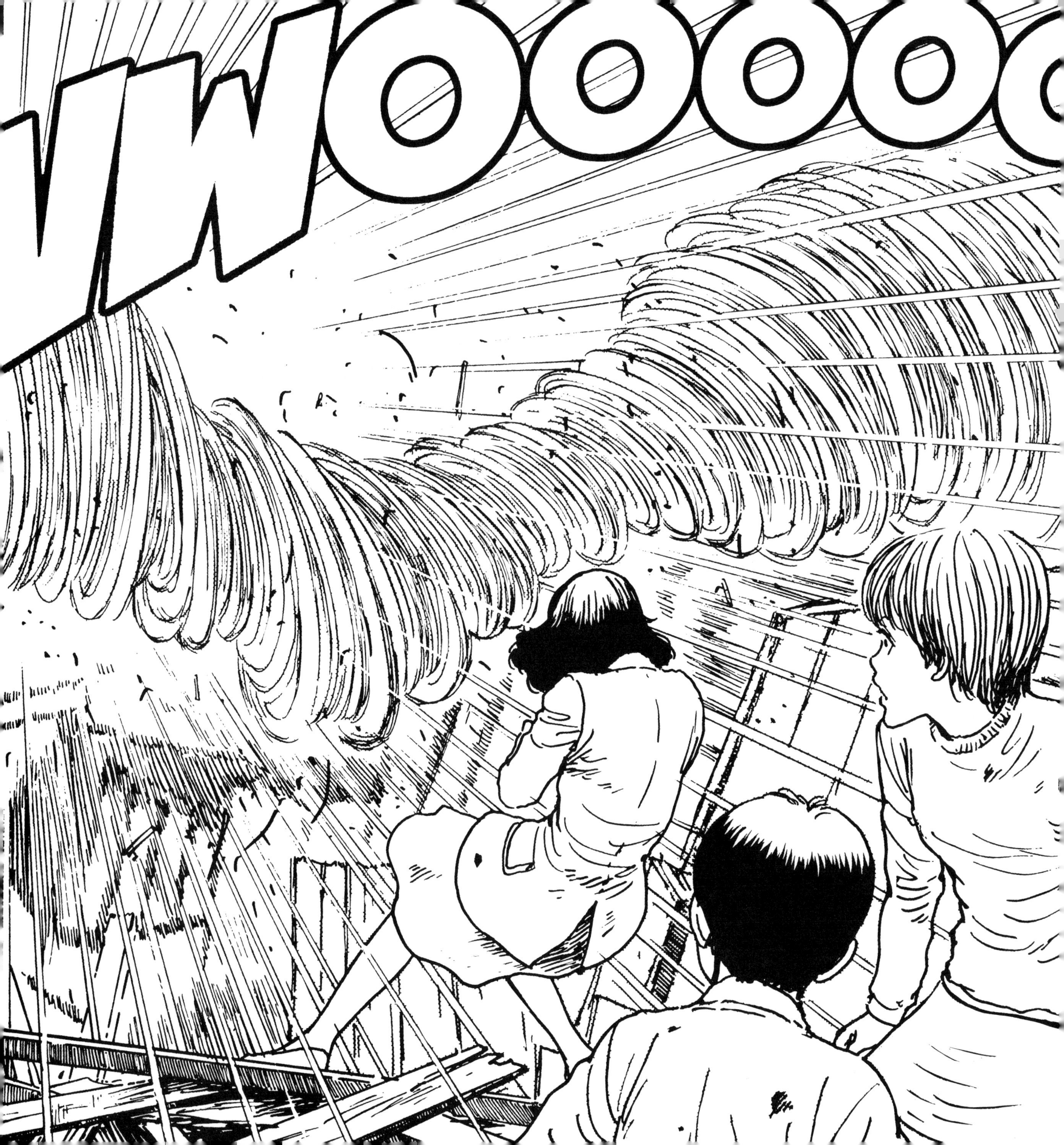
VWOOOOO

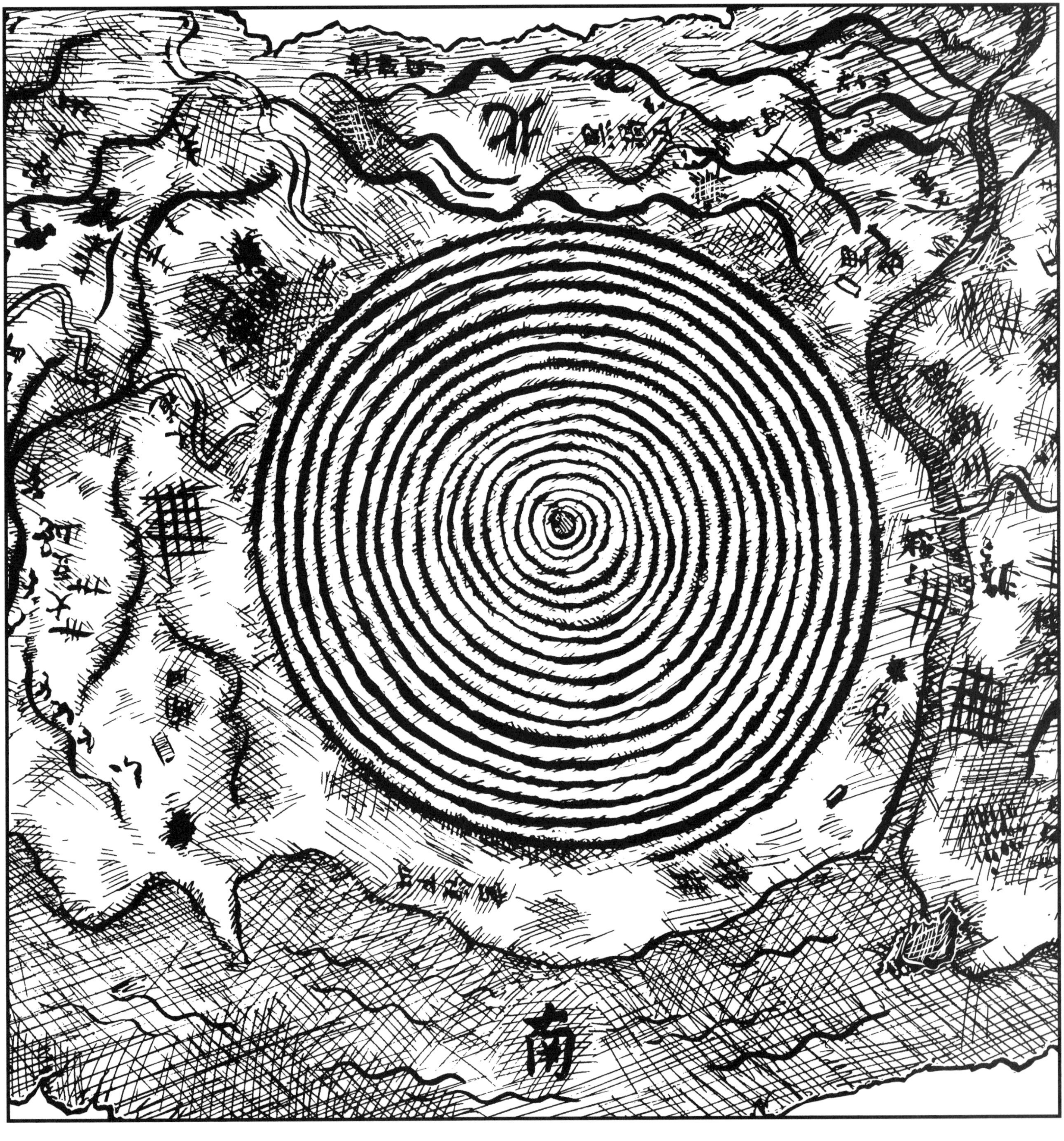
南

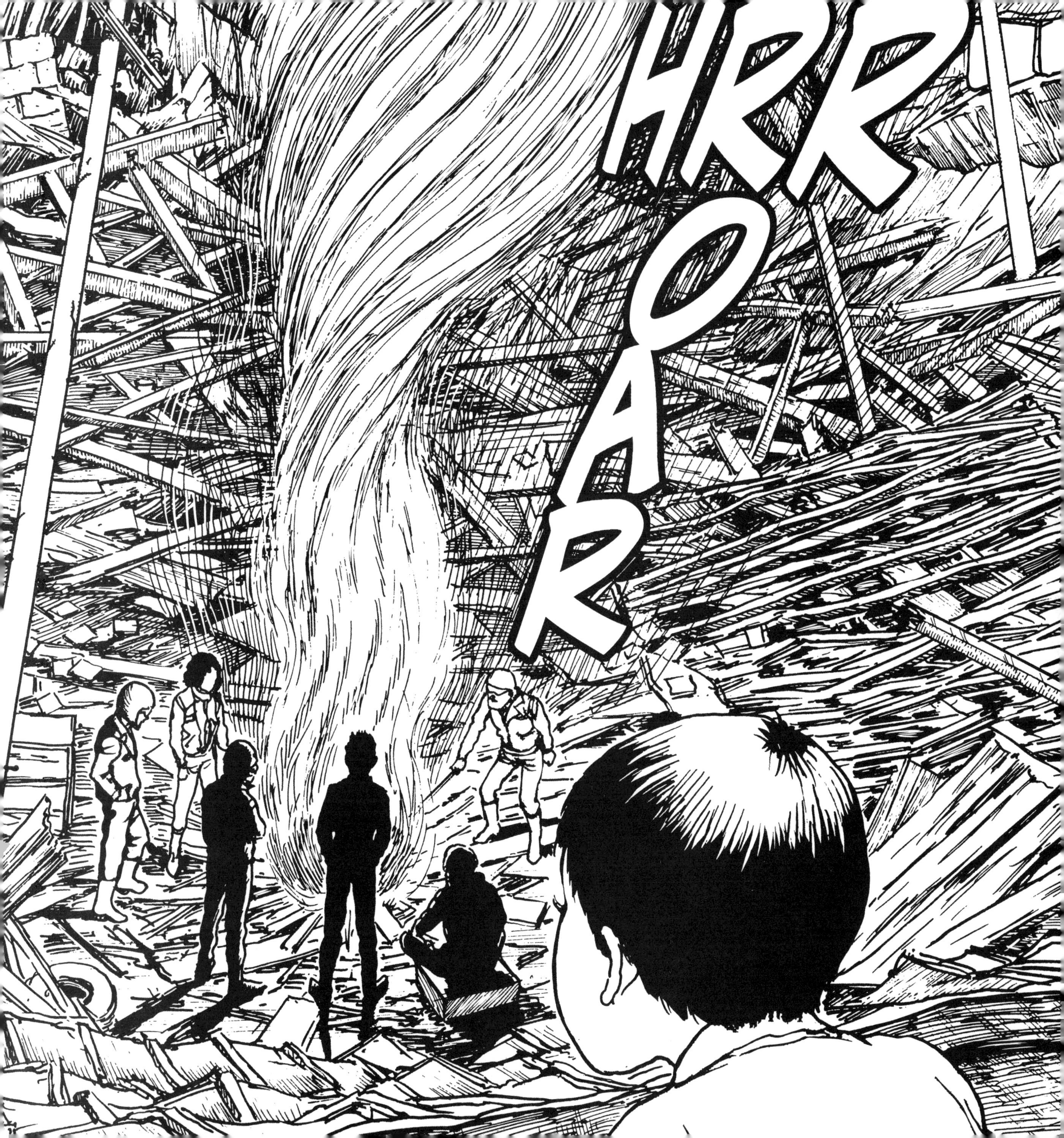
HRRROAR

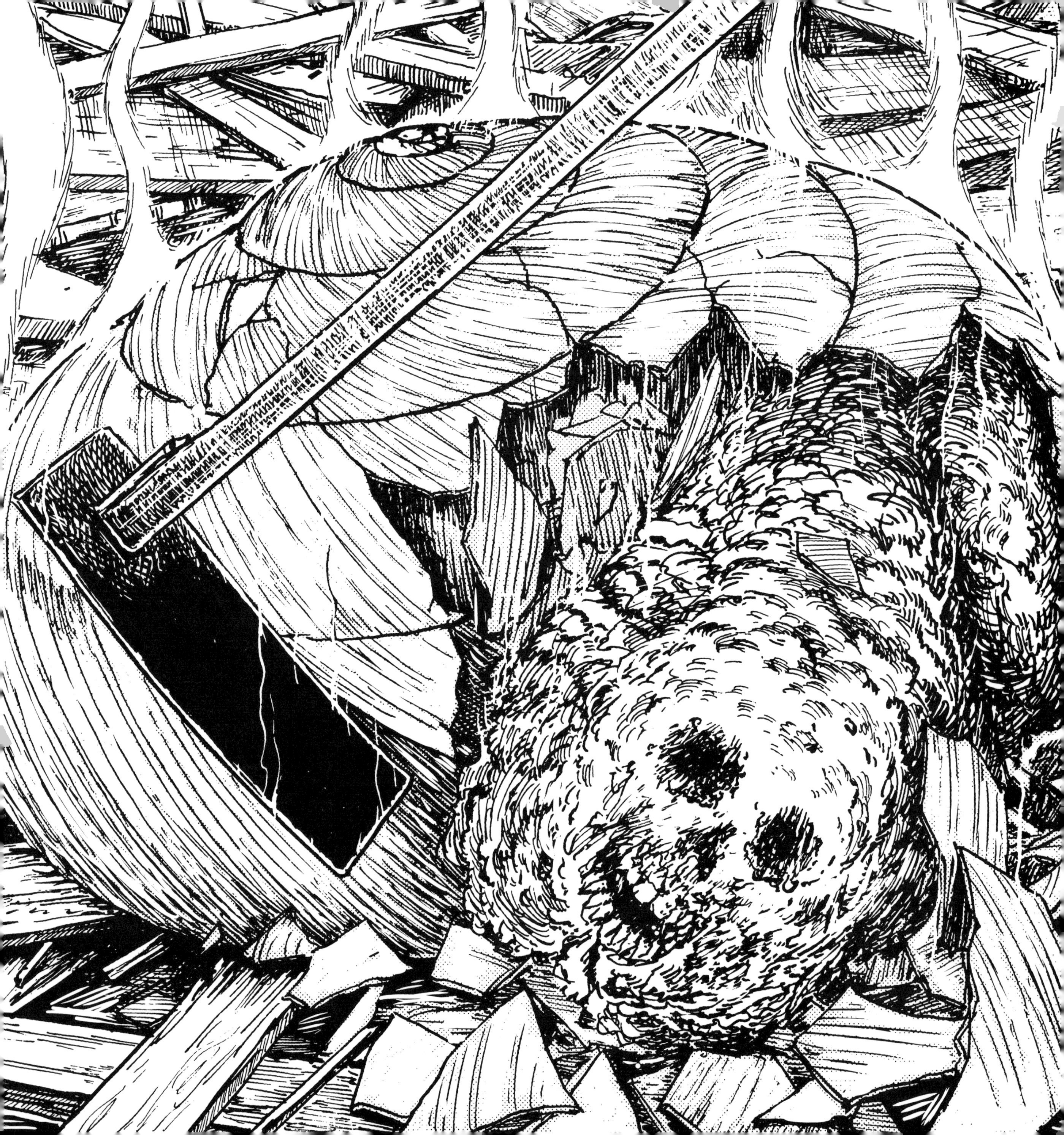

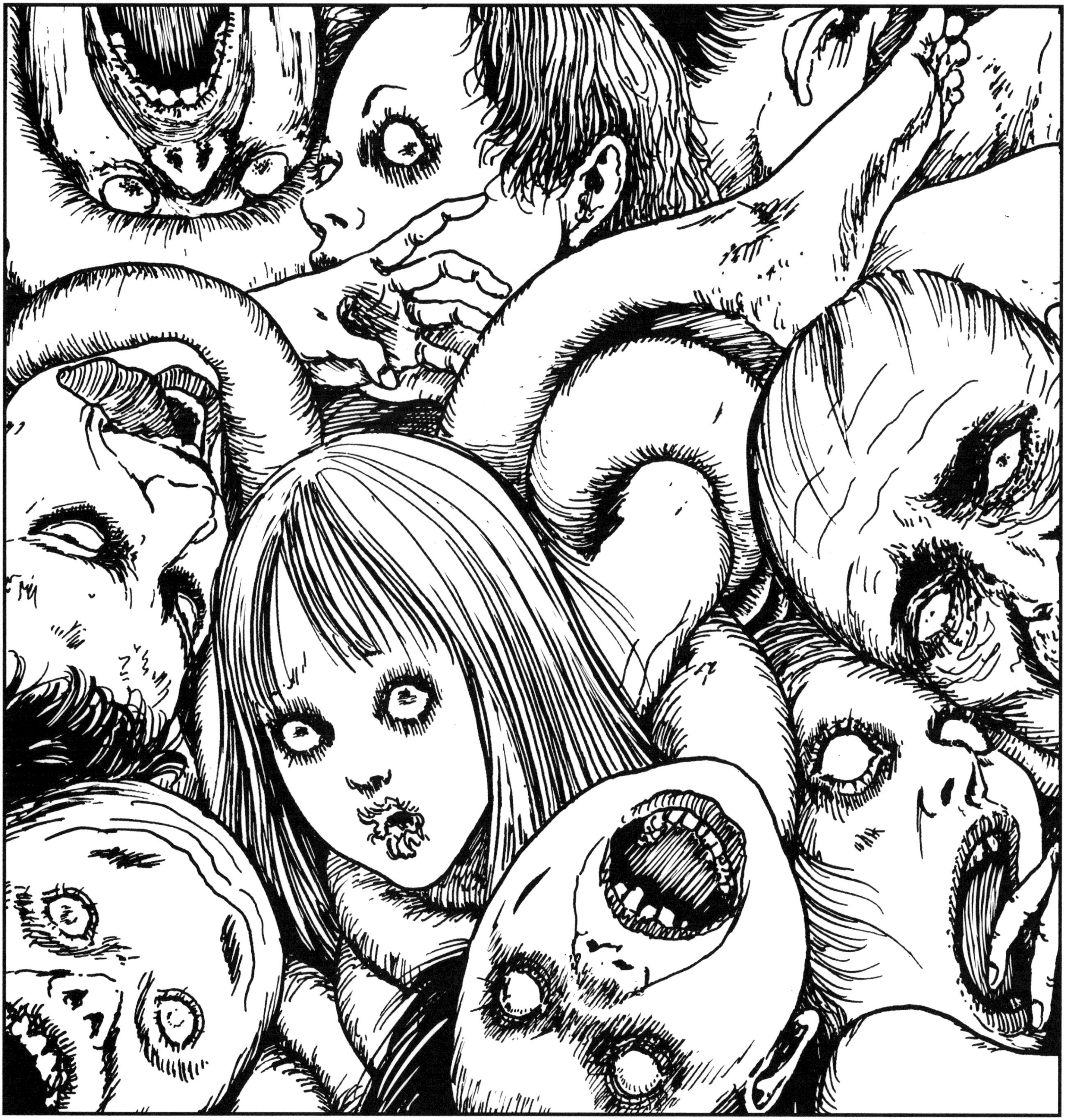

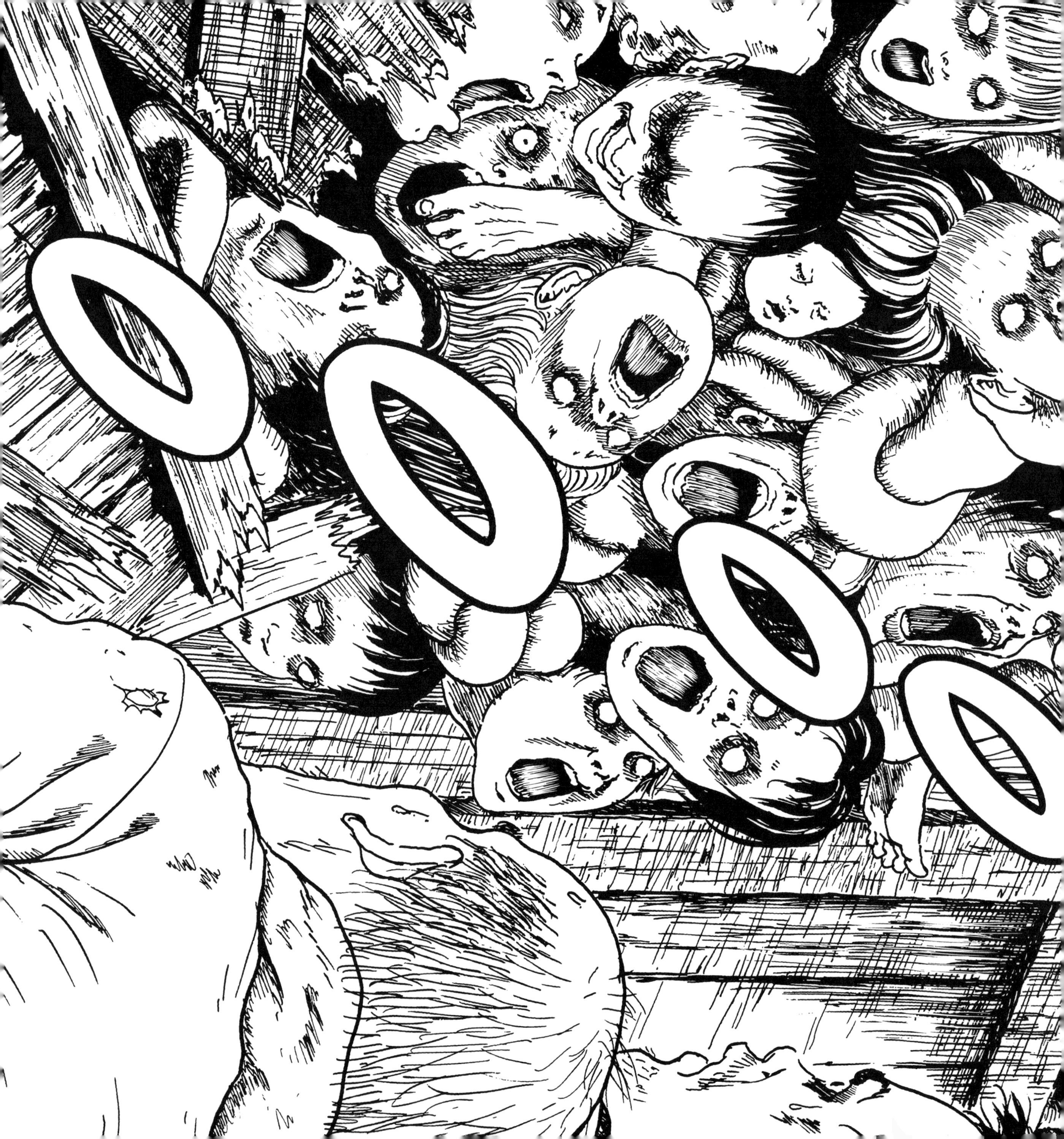

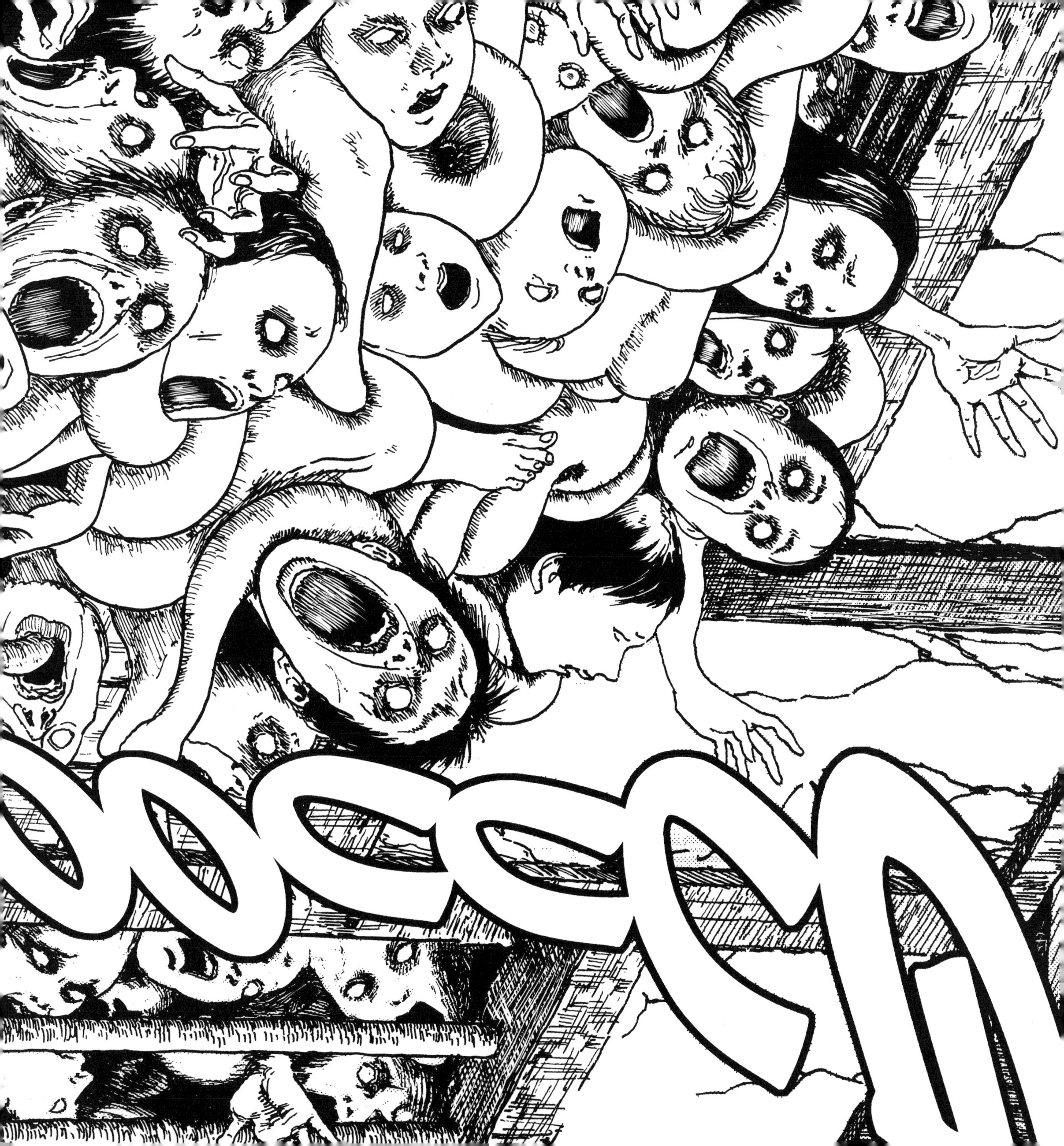

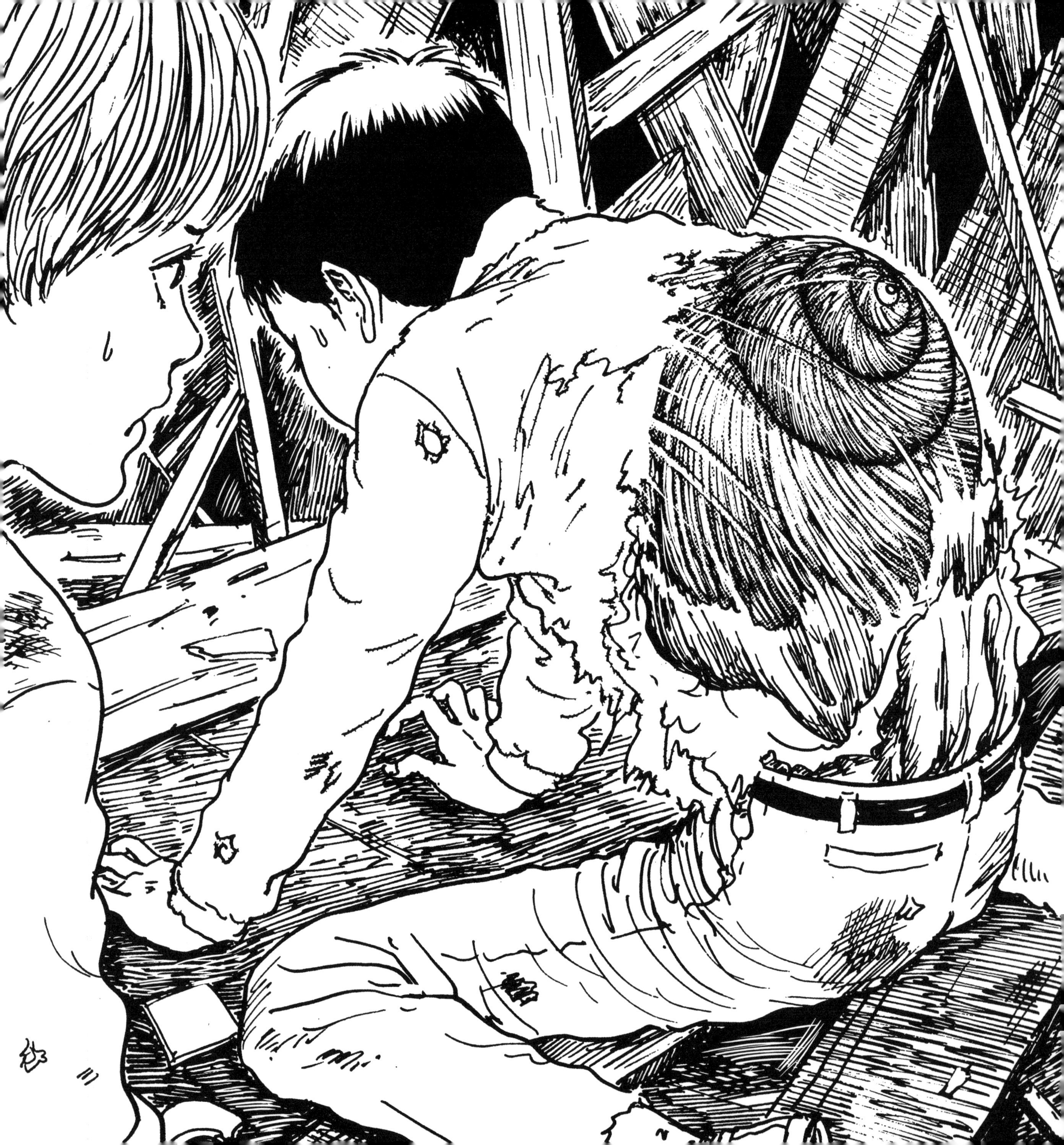

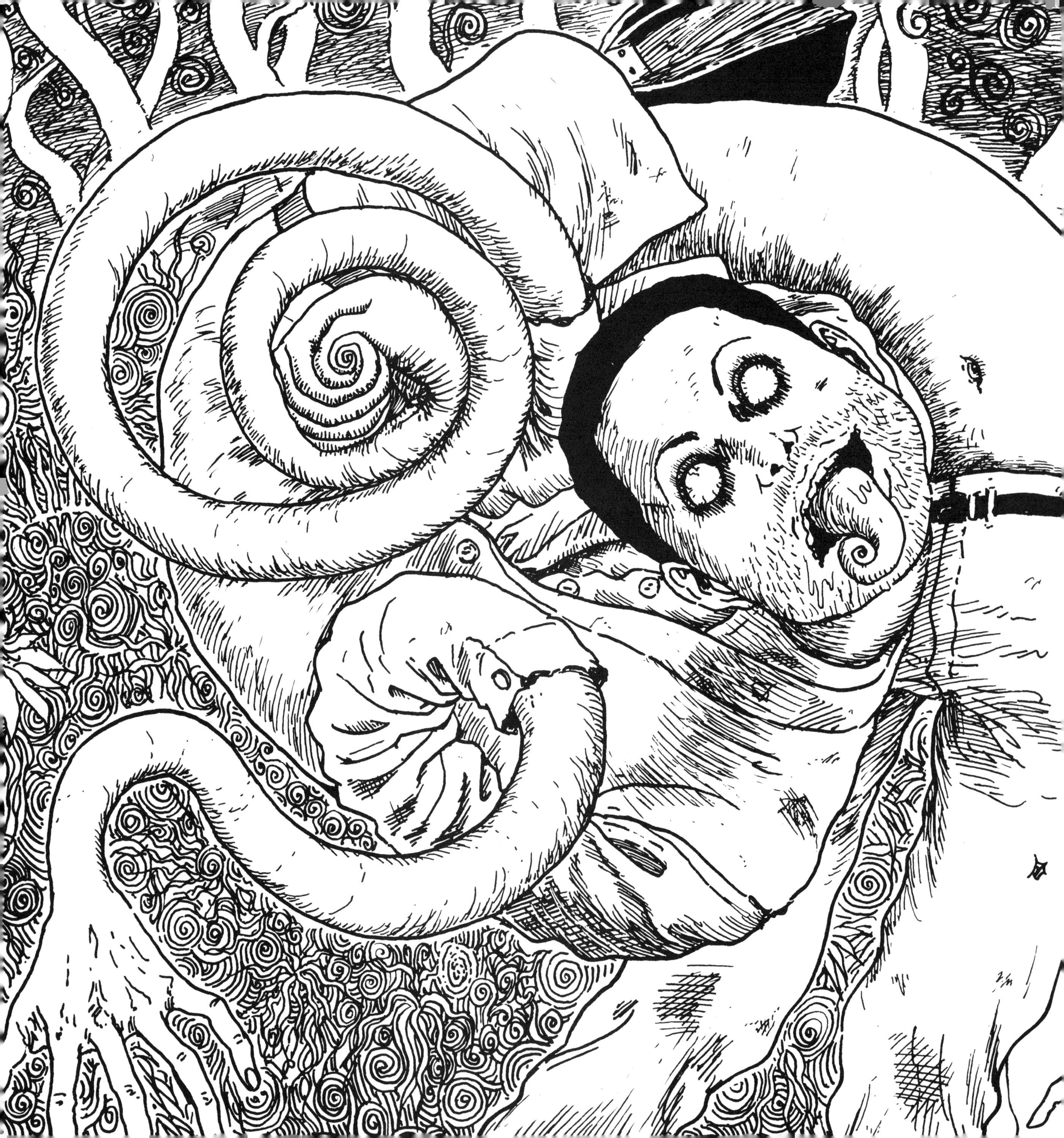

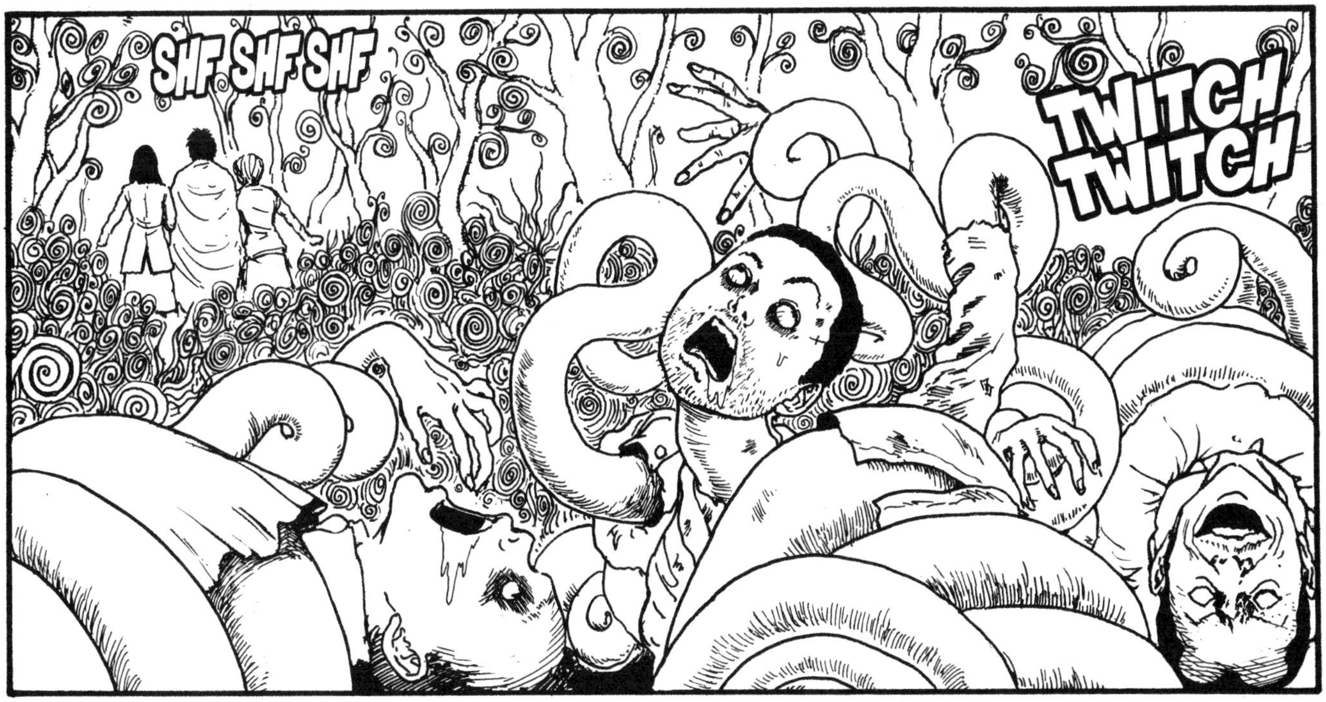
SHF SHF SHF
TWITCH TWITCH

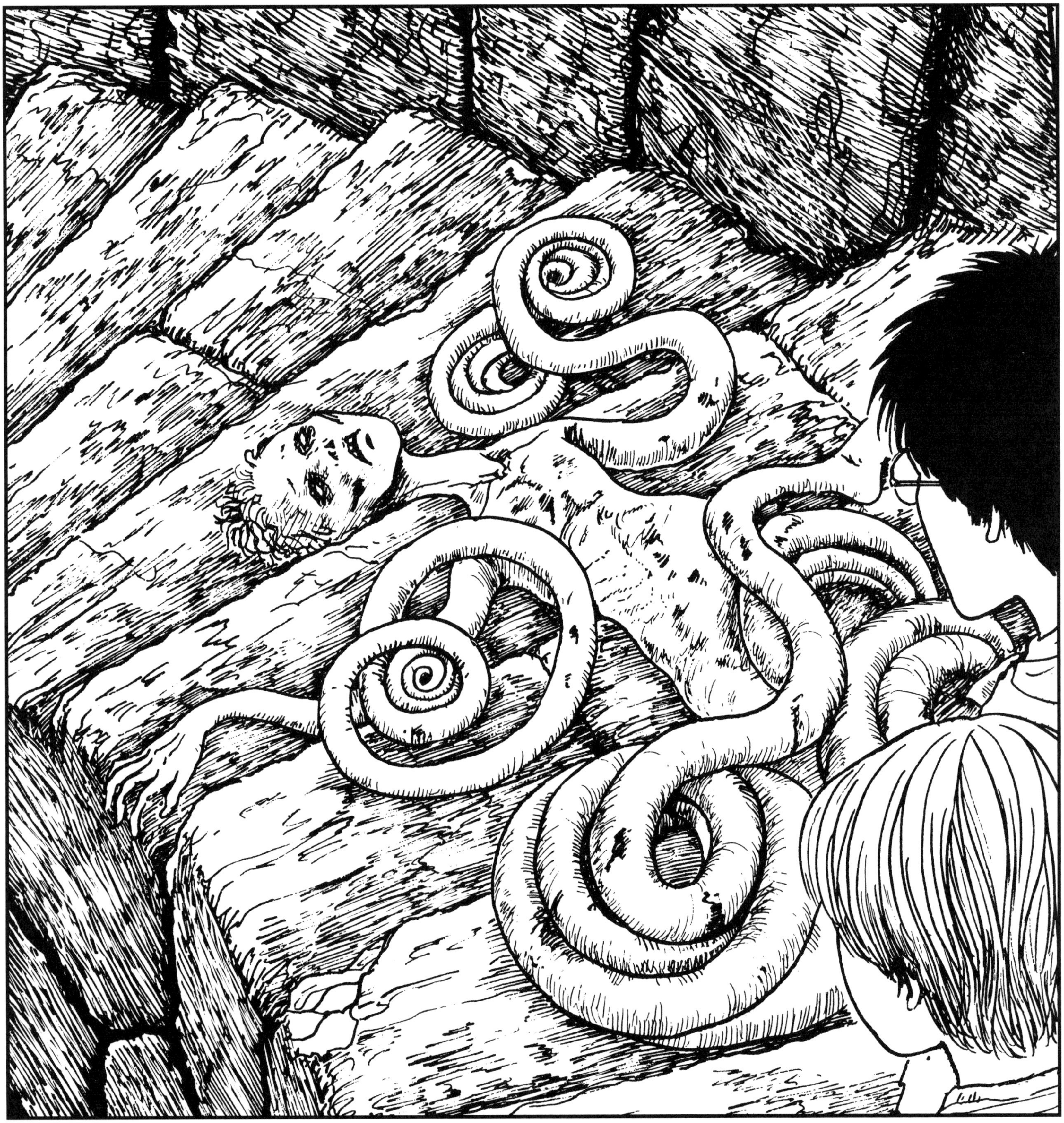

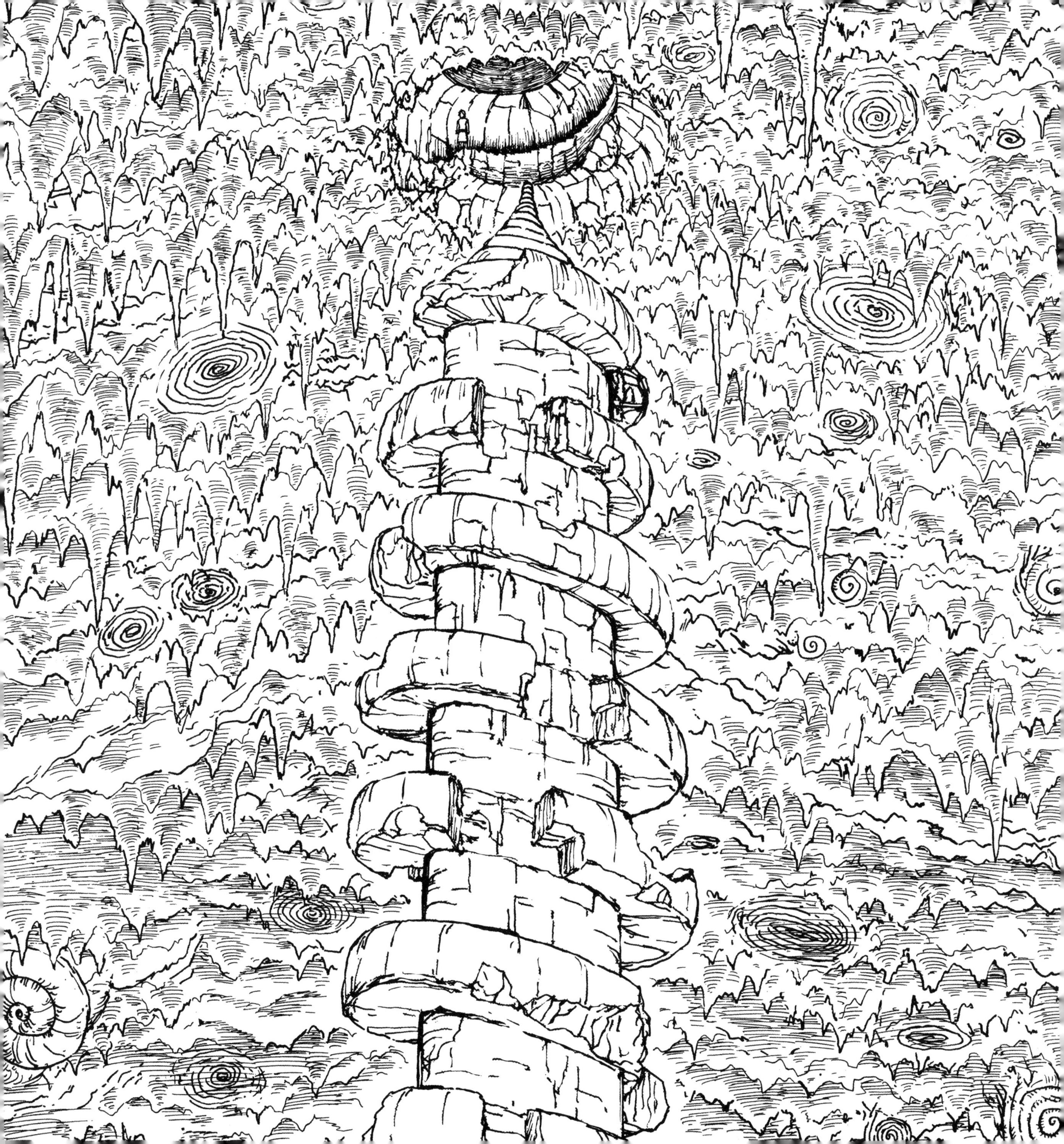

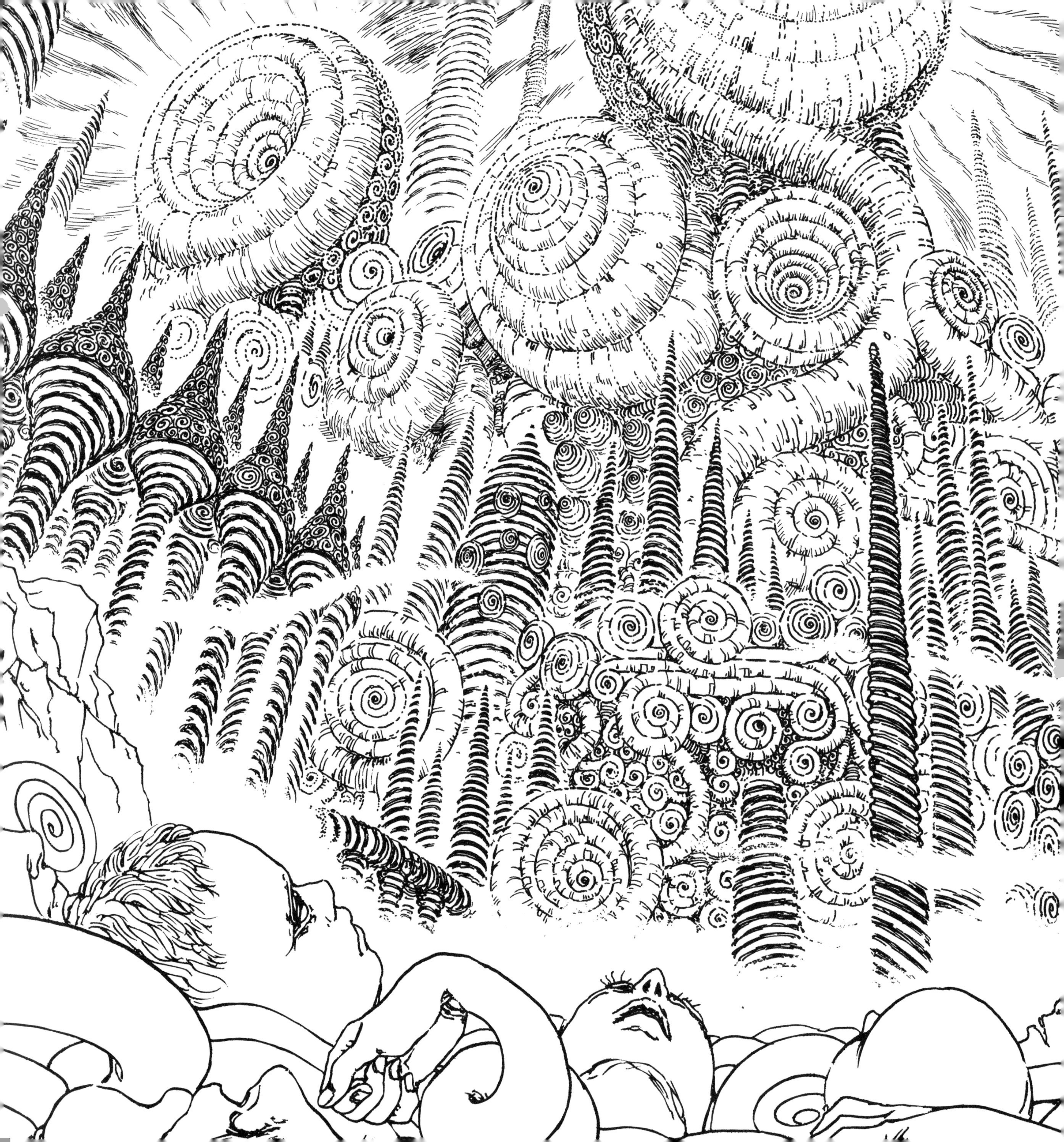

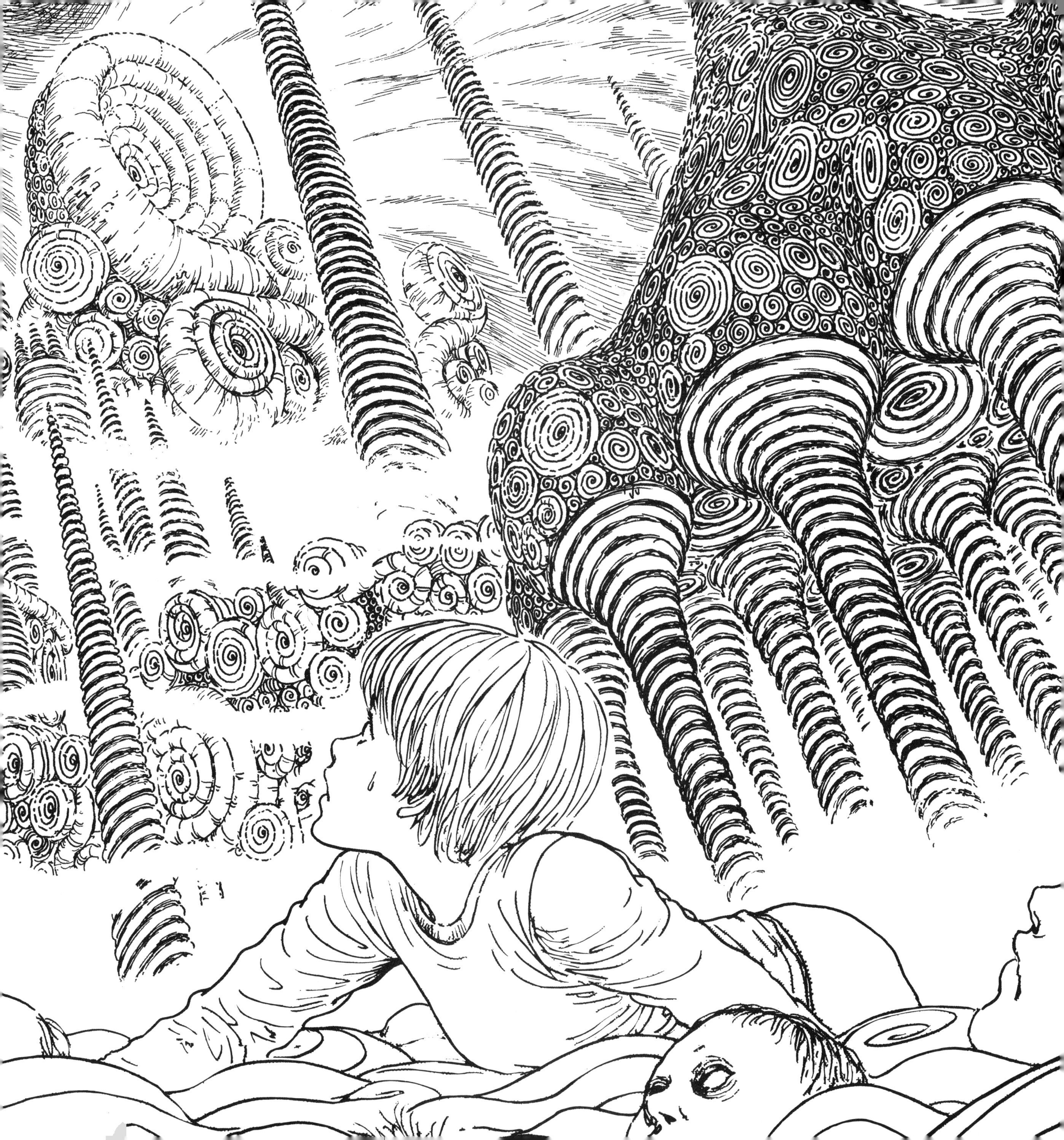

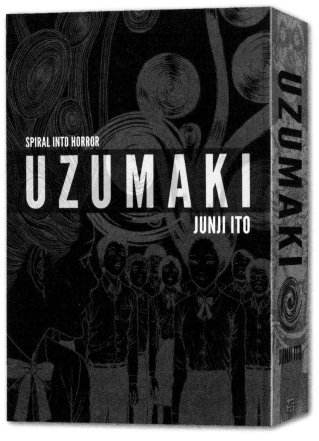

UZUMAKI

STORY AND ART BY JUNJI ITO

SPIRALS...
THIS TOWN IS CONTAMINATED WITH SPIRALS...

Kurouzu-cho, a small fogbound town on the coast of Japan, is haunted not by a person or being but a pattern: **UZUMAKI**, the spiral—the hypnotic secret shape of the world. The bizarre masterpiece of horror manga by Junji Ito is available in a deluxe hardcover format.